Darkest Secrets of Film Directing:

How Successful Film Directors Overcome Hidden Traps

2nd Edition

Tom Marcoux

Feature Film Producer, Director, Actor
and Screenwriter

Book #4 in the nine volume series
Darkest Secrets by Tom Marcoux

A QuickBreakthrough Publishing Edition

Copyright © 2013 Tom Marcoux Media, LLC
ISBN: 061581302X
ISBN-13: 978-0615813028

All rights reserved. No part of this book may be reproduced or transmitted in any form by any means electronic or mechanical, including photocopying, recording or by any information storage and retrieval system without written permission from the publisher.

QuickBreakthrough Publishing is an imprint of Tom Marcoux Media, LLC. More copies are available from the publisher, Tom Marcoux Media, LLC. Please call (415) 572-6609 or write TomSuperCoach@gmail.com

or visit www.TomSuperCoach.com

or Tom's blog: www.BeHeardandBeTrusted.com

This book was developed and written with care. Names and details were modified to respect privacy.

Disclaimer: The author and publisher acknowledge that each person's situation is unique, and that readers have full responsibility to seek consultations with health, financial, spiritual and legal professionals. The author and publisher make no representations or warranties of any kind, and the author and publisher shall not be liable for any special, consequential or exemplary damages resulting, in whole or in part, from the reader's use of, or reliance upon, this material.:

Other Books by Tom Marcoux:
- Darkest Secrets of Charisma
- Darkest Secrets of the Film and Television Industry Every Actor Should Know
- Darkest Secrets of Making a Pitch to the Film and Television Industry
- Darkest Secrets of Persuasion and Seduction Masters
- Darkest Secrets of Business Communication: Using Your Personal Brand
- Darkest Secrets of Small Business Marketing
- Darkest Secrets of Spiritual Seduction Masters
- Darkest Secrets of Negotiation Masters

Praise for *Darkest Secrets of Film Directing*:

"*Darkest Secrets of Film Directing* is a great course on the art and craft of film directing. It's especially helpful that Tom Marcoux reveals some important pitfalls you need to avoid."
– Danek S. Kaus, screenwriter and author of *Swords of the Dead*

"Tom consistently creates an environment where artists are encouraged to explore and discover the material, without compromising his own vision of the project. By allowing everyone to bring their best ideas to the table, Tom creates an environment that allows good work to thrive." – Dan Wilson, actor, director, producer

"When casting, film director Tom Marcoux's acting and improvisation skills shine as he works with actors."
– Daniel Buhlman, film director and actor

"Tom treats cast and crew with great respect. He listens to ideas. His support helped me express the truth in my scenes."
– David MacDowell Blue, actor, screenwriter and author of *The Annotated Carmilla*

Praise for Tom Marcoux's Other Work

"In *Darkest Secrets of Persuasion and Seduction Masters*, learn useful countermeasures to protect you from being darkly manipulated."
– David Barron, co-author, *Power Persuasion*

"In *Be Heard and Be Trusted*, Tom's advice on how to remain true to yourself and establish authentic rapport with clients is both insightful and reality based. He [shows how] to establish oneself as a credible expert."
-Arthur P. Ciaramicoli, Ed.D., Ph.D., author *The Curse of the Capable*, and *The Power of Empathy*

"*Nothing Can Stop You This Year* is a treasure trove of tips, tools, and terrific ideas—practical, reassuring, and energizing! Tom provides wonderful resources for achieving your goals." – Elayne Savage, Ph.D., author of *Don't Take It Personally! The Art of Dealing with Rejection*

Visit Tom's blog: www.BeHeardandBeTrusted.com

Tom Marcoux

CONTENTS

Dedication and Acknowledgments	i
Section One: 21 Darkest Secrets of the Film Directing (and Your Countermeasures)	1
Section Two: Use the D.I.R.E.C.T. System	115
Section Three: Make the Screenplay Excellent	121
Section Four: Develop the Film Project	139
Section Five: Preproduction	167
Section Six: Production	179
Section Seven: Post Production	182
Section Eight: Marketing—Fundraising—Distribution	189
A Final Word and Springboard to Your Dreams	194
Excerpt from *Darkest Secrets of the Film and Television Industry Every Actor Should Know: A Film Director and Actor Reveals Secrets for Your Acting, Auditions, Movie Roles and Self-promotion*	197
About the Author Tom Marcoux	207
Special Offer Just for Readers of this Book	209

DEDICATION AND ACKNOWLEDGEMENTS

This book is dedicated to the terrific book and film consultant, and author Johanna E. Mac Leod. It is also dedicated to the other team members. Thanks to David MacDowell Blue, Danek S. Kaus and Joan Harrison for editing. Thanks to my father, Al Marcoux, for his concern and efforts for me. Thanks to my mother, Sumiyo Marcoux, a kind, generous soul. Thanks to Daniel Buhlman for the cover photography and rendering this book's front cover. Thank you Johanna E. Mac Leod for rendering this book's back cover. Thank you to casting director Randi Acton for her insightful comments in the enclosed interview. Thank you to Higher Power. Thanks to our readers, audiences, clients, my graduate/college students and my team members of Tom Marcoux Media, LLC.

SECTION ONE:
21 DARKEST SECRETS OF FILM DIRECTING (AND YOUR COUNTERMEASURES) —CHAPTER 1

What do you hope for with your film directing career? Do you want to make blockbuster films or intimate dramas? Are you looking forward to hearing an audience's laughter in all the right places?

From my experiences directing feature films and other projects, I know directing is at once exciting and scary. You're both an artist and a leader. A big part of leadership consists of preparing for what lies ahead—getting ready for surprises, while trying your best to make sure nothing surprises you. It works for art. It works for business. And it works for making movies. I wrote this book to alert you, to warn you about filmmaking traps and how you can plan countermeasures ahead of time.

Director James Cameron said, "You have to not listen to the nay sayers because there will be many and often they'll be much more qualified than you and cause you to sort of doubt yourself." But this book is about the exact opposite—saying "yes" to yourself. Yes, you can overcome the hidden traps. Yes, you can manage the problems that pop up daily. Yes, you most certainly can direct that film which is a cherished dream.

Sprinkled throughout this book you'll find comments from 30 top film directors (Spielberg to Kurosawa, Spike Lee to Quentin Tarantino and beyond).

Many filmmakers choose that path because of certain movies: Movies that inspire, and move, and make us want to see more. From there they decide to actually make that "more" themselves. Too often, they find the mechanics and frustrations of the industry daunting. Hope gives way to dwindled dreams and ambitions left by the road. Let me, with this book, be helpful. Let me keep your hopes alive.

Director Kathryn Bigelow said, "I believe there's hope, because the breakdown and the repair are happening simultaneously."

Bigelow was describing film subject matter, but she could also be describing filmmaking itself.

Let's begin.

DARKEST SECRET #1: SOME OF YOUR BEST IDEAS WON'T WORK.

George Takei (Lieutenant—later Captain—Sulu of *Star Trek* fame) saved me from a bad scene I had written for a feature film I was directing.

When I met him to discuss a role, he proved gracious. More, the man is funny. His laughter turned out warm and resounding.

I showed some storyboards. One depicted a barely lit scene. One in the morning and our hero sheds a single tear. That single teardrop falls into his tea cup. As it strikes the surface, the teardrop makes a tidal wave in the tea, splashing a tiny tsunami within its porcelain walls. It was like a comet falling into the ocean, but in miniature. All in close up. Extreme close up. Slow motion, too.

At the time, I was so proud of that.

"Uh, Tom?" George asked gently. "Isn't that a bit melodramatic?"

Of course in retrospect I see that scene was a bit melodramatic the same way the North Pole in winter is a bit chilly. I took George's advice and cut the scene. Later, my film gained a distributor, went to the Cannes film market and earned international distribution.

First cuts are a bitch for a director, because it's been so many months and you put your trust in your editor and you're going to see your film assembled for the first time. You look at it and go, This is terrible. I hate it. - Richard Donner (director of Superman *and* Lethal Weapon*)*

Avoid growling at people who give you feedback. It's like a friend who tells you to remove the spinach on your teeth before you go into a job interview. Or it can be. Depends on who they are. In time you learn to discern whose input makes sense, improves your work. Others won't understand. They'll have nothing worthwhile to offer. Usually. But sometimes a strange idea can spark an improvement. Hence the vital need to encourage feedback and listen to the feedback given (even if you ignore it).

Encourage people to share their opinions. For example, I say things like:

"I'm glad you brought that up" and "I'm going to really think about that." Even at times when I want to scream defenses for my first ideas. Sometimes my ideas work and sometimes they bear improving.

Steven Spielberg said, "Directing is knowing when to say 'yes.'"

I'll add that directing is also making an atmosphere so people feel comfortable and contribute and you'll be saying 'yes' often. Remain approachable. For example, when actors want to try a take in unusual ways, say, "Let's try it."

Points to Remember:

Darkest Secret #1: Some of your best ideas won't work.

Your Countermeasure:
You don't have to take anyone's advice, but hearing more thoughts gives you more options.

Tom Marcoux

CHAPTER 2
DARKEST SECRET #2: SOME "FILMMAKING MYTHS" CAN REALLY SCREW YOU UP.

On the set watching Chris O'Donnell run in and toss something into a fake mailbox, I was an actor not the director. The director was competent and he achieved his objectives. At some moments, stray thoughts about where I'd put the camera arose in my mind. Director or not, I had an opinion. Trust me, on the set, there are a lot of opinions.

Screenwriting teachers get the opportunity to pronounce their opinions as "rules." Each semester, they discuss these "rules"—which I sometimes call "filmmaking myths." Here is one: "Never use narration."

As a screenwriter, I realize that using narration can be like a crutch. But wait a minute. Some of the most successful and appreciated films of all time include narration. *To Kill A Mockingbird, The Shawshank Redemption, The Man Who Would Be King, It's A Wonderful Life, The Princess Bride, Henry V, Bram Stoker's Dracula* as well as *The Lord of the Rings*.

If your film seems to require narration, don't let some pronouncement in a classroom stop you. I learned this the hard way. Years ago, I screened a rough cut of one of my films for an acquaintance, a producer. He suggested I consider adding narration. My training as a screenwriter conditioned me to dismiss the idea. Now with hindsight, I realize the humbling truth. I could have improved the film. Narration would have provided bridges between scenes. And the most important detail: the narration would have encouraged the audience to care about the characters and story. If audience members feel confused, they may not feel connected to the characters. Narration would have solved that problem.

Another filmmaking myth: Never use flashbacks. This is another rule screenwriting teachers love to emphasize. But I recently saw an episode of the TV series *Castle*. When the character Detective Kate Becket flashes back to memories of the day she was shot, you viscerally feel her agony and fear.

Finally, another "myth": Never use a nightmare to fake out the audience. One of the creepiest film moments I have ever seen occurs in the TV mini-series *Bag of Bones*, based on the Stephen King novel that I read some years ago. Our main character Mike Noonan (portrayed by Pierce Brosnan) lays back in bed and hears a scratching sound from beneath his bed. Soon he looks under the bed and sees his wife dragged into the darkness. Her fingernails are scraping on the carpet. Then he wakes up. It was a nightmare and emphasizes his torment in the wake of his wife's death.

As we direct a film, we must ready ourselves to drop our preconceptions and "go where the film leads." Each film blossoms and changes as we make it. And we need to do what's right for that film. Avoid letting rules lead you by the nose. Why? Because you are the artist. Not a book you read once nor some teacher in a class. Ideas we hear are just that ideas. Sometimes they help and sometimes they hinder. Take a quiet moment and listen to your intuition.

Points to Remember:

Darkest Secret #2: Some "filmmaking myths" can really screw you up.

Your Countermeasure:
Remember, you are the artist. Take a quiet moment and listen to your intuition.

Tom Marcoux

CHAPTER 3
DARKEST SECRET #3: BE A DIRECTOR FIRST, A FRIEND SECOND.

A director must be a policeman, a midwife, a psychoanalyst, a sycophant and a bastard. - Billy Wilder, director of Some Like It Hot *and* The Apartment

A film director has to get a shot, no matter what he does. We're desperate people. - Elia Kazan, director of On the Waterfront *and* A Streetcar Named Desire

Directing movies is a tough job. You must pull everyone together and tame the "wild film." At times, you'll feel your job is herding cats rather than making art or entertainment.

So you cannot be everyone's friend. Why? Because every day, you're going to make a decision, one that will disappoint someone. How? Your director of photography will want to lay tracks for a complicated shot, but you'll know that your actors are getting tired and you'll probably lose the light before you get a solid take. Or perhaps, your costume designer will want to add a special flare to an actor's wardrobe, but you know that it will be distracting in Scene 62.

Sometimes, you can mollify someone—like shooting an extra take so that an actor can try his wild idea.

But you're going to have to overrule some department head at some time.

You need to be a director first, a friend second. Let's look at some of the different elements:

A director
- demonstrates competence, confidence and caring
- leads

A friend
- protects a person's feelings
- sometimes shows vulnerability

Truly, these elements are not always mutually exclusive, but your duties as the director must come first.

A director demonstrates competence.

Do your homework. Know the script better than anyone else including the writer. For example, before I directed my first feature film, I personally sketched 803 storyboards. I knew the film backwards and forwards. Do your research. Take copious notes and identify your original intentions for the film and each individual scene.

A director demonstrates confidence.

Body language forms much of what people interpret as confidence. To demonstrate confidence, you'll do well by dropping distracting behaviors that scream "nervous person here!" What behaviors? Talking too fast, rubbing your hands, and allowing your body to be out of alignment.

1) *Talking too fast.* Pause to take a relaxed breath. Convey an idea in few words and then pause and breathe. This will help you avoid the nervous-sounding non-words like "um," "ah" or "uh." When you pause, you let the person take in your comment.

2) *Rubbing your hands.* I say, "Don't pet the cat"—that is, sometimes people comfort themselves by petting one hand with the other—as if one hand was a cat. This behavior reeks of fear. Simply use your peripheral vision to see what your hands are doing. If you catch yourself rubbing your hands, do something different. Perhaps, hold a pen. Or jot a note in a notebook. Or simply keep your hands away from each other.

3) *Allowing your body to be out of alignment.* Have you ever seen someone only half-turn toward a person who asks a question? What does this convey on the subconscious level? There are a number of possibilities, including "I don't care about you or what you're saying." However, there can be a worst impression. Author Joe Navarro, a former FBI agent, notes that special agents watch people's feet, hands and face—in that order. If you're not aligned with someone who asks a question, your feet might be saying, "I want to run away." What is the solution? Something I call: "Heart faces heart." Fully turn toward the person and have your heart face her heart. This action demonstrates your interest and your personal confidence.

Here is a special detail if you're of average or small stature. I learned this method from Lynda Obst, producer of *Sleepless in Seattle* and *Contact*. She said, "Take up more space." How do you do that? You gesture in wider movements. You also hold yourself with good posture.

Imagine that a string from the ceiling is attached to your spine and pulls you up so that all of your vertebrae align.

A director demonstrates caring.

How do you demonstrate that you're caring and concerned? You ask gentle questions and listen. For example, if you see that an actor is irritable, you could ask, "George, what can I set up today to make your job easier?" Keep in mind George might ask for something impossible. Be ready to tell him that. If he catches you lying to him, or thinking you're lying, you might as well start scratching your camera lens with a razor blade. But if he sees you try to accommodate him, he'll probably remember. If you can do what he asks, and then you actually go ahead, George may never forget! More, he'll tell people. Most of them will like what they hear.

Even if you cannot fulfill a request, people appreciate being asked. Significant research backs this up. People will do better when asked what would help—even if nothing changes. They appreciate that someone is paying attention.

A director leads.

The actors want to trust you. They want to know that you'll protect them.

Some things you know about, you know what the ingredients are—maybe not all of them. But it's up to you to put in the amount. It's up to the director to nag you until you get it right.
- Judi Dench, actress

Ms. Dench used the word "nag." I sometimes say that a director needs to lead or to push people. Francis Ford Coppola is known for saying, "Good. Let's do it again" as he calls for multiple takes.

When you lead, you do not need to issue orders. You can use informal words like:
- Good. Let's try it this way . . .
- Sam, how about you find a moment where you pick up that clock . . .
- Marina, I feel that we're missing an opportunity here. What else can you find in the moment when you're confronting Frieda?

Here's one of my favorite moments of directing a feature film. During one scene, the lead actor portraying "John" jumped ahead in emotions and was sad and heartbroken from the first words of his dialogue. I invited him to be in "happy memory time" when he talked about meeting a girl. Then he had some place to go when he got to the part:

"Then, I lost her. And our baby. [sadness]
I finally found them in a refugee camp. [a moment of joy]
Then Kim got sick. And she died. . . God . . ." [a plunge into despair]

After the lead actor did the scene using my suggestion, he was all smiles. He said, "Tom, that was a great note!" He needed to experience the scene; then he understood.

Ms. Dench may call it "nagging"—but I call directing leading and facilitating.

Some people say that certain directors are charismatic. To be charismatic, demonstrate that you care about your team. Charisma is not about impressing people as to how great you are. It's about encouraging people and helping them unleash how great they are.

They'll love you for it!

Points to Remember:

Darkest Secret #3: Be a director first, a friend second.

Your Countermeasure:
Learn to lead. Be prepared that you will make decisions that will disappoint some people. Learn to ask gentle questions and listen—and people will get the impression you're caring, concerned and competent.

CHAPTER 4
DARKEST SECRET #4: PEOPLE WILL GET ANGRY. DEAL WITH IT.

Director Michael Mann (*Ali, Collateral*) said, "Every actor is totally different. . . . My director-to-actor language is completely unique and different for every single actor I talk to. Because Val Kilmer works differently than Tom Cruise, than Jamie Fox and Al Pacino, DeNiro, Daniel Day Lewis. Everybody works completely different. . . . All of these people are highly committed, very artistically ambitious, as am I. . . . It's usually a relationship where two people are very aggressively trying to get to a defined point in space that is very difficult to get to."

These are powerful words and actions: "highly committed, artistically ambitious, aggressively trying to get to a defined point." The process implies that the director, actor, director of photography (among others) all have ambitions. Of course, they're going to come into conflict. If someone else appears to prevail, a number of people get irritable or downright angry when they feel thwarted from getting what they want. What do you do?

Here are five techniques to effectively deal with conflict:

Technique #1: Meet the person's emotional tone.

Avoid saying "calm down." Why? Because the person is committed to their goals and feels, "Of course, I'm upset. This is important!"

Saying "Calm down" comes across as an insult. What you're coming across as saying is

"You're losing control" or worse, "This is a trivial situation so there's no need to be upset."

How do you deal with this? You match the person's emotional tone (intense) while saying something like: "Yes! I hear how important this is to you. It sounds so frustrating."

Technique #2: Gradually reduce the intensity of your own tone.

After you have met the person's tone with a matching tone, start to gradually quiet down and perhaps, slow down the rate of your speech. In this manner, you are leading the person to quiet down.

Cinematographer: No! A long trucking shot would be perfect here!

Director: Yes! That would be a great shot!

Cinematographer: Then let's do it.

Director: I want to do it. [start lowering the intensity of the tone]

Cinematographer: Great. I'll get my crew to start now.

Director: I don't know if you heard—this is [name actor's] last day. We just got to pick up more coverage. [continue lowering the intensity of the tone].

This "gradually reducing the intensity of your own tone"

method takes practice. See if you can rehearse with a trusted friend.

Technique #3: Take a deep breath.
Sometimes, when a team member is angry, it sounds like they're personally attacking (sometimes they are). Take a deep breath. Pause before you say anything.

Technique #4: Go neutral.
Someone yells. What do we do? Yell back or back away. That's a reaction. If we yell back, it's natural. We're defending ourselves. Or we back away. Hope for the latter is a big reason yelling starts in the first place. It is a way of winning. Yelling back usually translates into escalation, each side trying to make the other back down. Understandable. We all like to win. But on the set (as well as in life) neither response really translates into winning. Because either way you've lost control.

Instead, "going neutral" is a powerful response you can make. Remaining unflappable is the epitome of control. Self control. This is not indifference. Failure to respond at all is nearly always a mistake. The problem gets ignored and people nearby start to worry if you pay attention, whether you even can pay attention.

Let's say an actor Sam yells about something. The director "Miranda" says, "I'm listening, Sam. What's going on?" This is a "going neutral" response. Miranda avoids placating Sam, and she does not ignore his upset. She also avoids saying, "Calm down, Sam. It's no big deal."

Listen, respond appropriately to the problem, and let it go. Among other things, you'll gain a reputation for a calm head. People will say you're reliable. That you can be counted on to get things done and avoid drama.

Better yet, all those things they'll be saying about you? They'll be true.

Technique #5: Avoid meeting emotion with logic
"You can't logic me out of how I feel. I get to feel the way I feel." Those words have come out of my mouth. More than once. Usually to a family member. Maybe you've said something similar. Or heard it said. Maybe not. But almost everyone has thought it, whether they realize it or not.

When people are upset, when their emotions are high, when their voice is cracking under the pressure of whatever-it-is they are feeling—they don't want to hear a lecture. Neither do you. In fact, a lecture sounds like condescension. Worse, it's evidence the listener didn't hear what was most important—how the speaker felt. At best a rational response to an emotional outburst seems like a non sequitur. Like someone asking for your phone number after hearing you've been shot. Worse, it can come across as dismissive, as if the speaker's emotions cannot have any import. Their love, their hate, their fear seems to be ignored.

This doesn't help.

But what does help is to help the speaker shift gears. Look them right in the eye and double-check what they just said. Actually ask them. Don't go through the motions. Repeat it again, this time honing in on something. Maybe exactly what they want in response or asking if something specific has set them off. The idea is to start by letting the speaker know you're listening. It sounds tricky, but you need to match him emotionally while remaining rational. Take his words absolutely seriously, repeat them (remember, that tells him you were listening) and give a rational response only slightly less intensely than his initial outburst.

Exactly what you say next depends on context, but the trick remains to slightly decrease your intensity each time you speak. At the same time, make it clear you're listening. Ask him to clarify what he just said. In effect, you're talking him down. This sounds complex, but in practice you'll find it many times easier than it seems. Often you'll find one or two sentences will do the trick.

Technique #6: Say, "That sounds [frustrating, painful, disappointing]."

Where does the anger come from? Fear. One primal fear we have is that no one understands us. And we're afraid of not being heard. (I wrote a book on this topic entitled *Be Heard and Be Trusted.*)

So say back to the person something that is appropriate like: "That sounds [frustrating, painful, disappointing]." When you say that something "sounds" or "sounds like" you are not "telling someone what they feel." You're actually expressing your guess as to what they're feeling. You're giving them space to feel what they feel.

Surprisingly, people often merely reply with something like: "Yeah. It is frustrating." You're validating the person's feelings. That effort does much to lower someone's level of feeling upset.

The love scenes that worked . . . were the ones where the actors weren't fearful. When somebody was fearful, you could see it right away. It takes you out of the story, and that's to be avoided at all costs. - Jennifer Beals, actress

Let's face it. People become angry when they're fearful. Imagine this situation: the role you're playing requires you to carry another actor, but you have a truly weak back.

Perhaps you can relate to this. I once strained my back by merely washing a bathtub. If you have a weak back, you know that it can cramp your whole day. Continued pain drains energy and makes people irritable.

The trouble is sometimes we're in a situation in which we feel trapped. For example, the actor who portrayed the robot Gort in the classic film *The Day the Earth Stood Still* had a weak back (as many tall people do). The actor was hired to be tall and strong. Fortunately, director Robert Wise customized the filming. If you see the film, you'll probably notice how Gort goes behind a wall and then shortly comes back with the lead actress Patricia Neal already in his arms. If you squint, you will likely notice that there are thin cables holding Ms. Neal up!

Actors can become angry and sometimes do not know the actual source of their fear. Look an actor deep in the eyes and say firmly, "What can I do?" If they dither, ask if they need some time. Or if they can pull it together for just a few minutes. You might say something like: "Would another take work for you? Then, I can get the crew setting up the next shot, and we can talk more." See if it's an appropriate time to give the actor a break.

I have noticed on film sets some actors and crew people show contempt for each other. For example, there's an infamous recording of actor Christian Bale on the set of *Terminator: Salvation*. It includes Bale's threats to quit the production. Apparently, the director of photography walked through the set during a take. In a meltdown that took four full minutes, Bale shouted a specific obscenity a total of thirty-nine times. Bale, at one point, yelled at the man, "Do you want me to go ——ing trash your lights? Do you want me to ——ing trash them? Then why are you trashing my scene? You do it one more ——ing time and I ain't walking on this set if you're still hired. I'm — —ing serious."

So what do you, as a director, do with a situation like that? Your job is to get the shots. You're the one everyone is looking to for leadership. Who do you lead first? Yourself.

First, don't match anger with anger. Calm yourself down. Better yet, remain calm from the start. Since you might at most have three whole seconds to respond once the star stops screaming at the top of his lungs, remaining calm is usually the better option.

I have shared six techniques in this section. And still, I'm concerned that you have methods that you can use in the heat of a conflict. Now, I'll share a way to remember useful techniques with four words: Breathe. Listen. Repeat. Move.

Now, I'll state the process in a few words:

Breathe. Retain your calm. Pause before you say anything.
Listen. Avoid interrupting if possible. Hear the person out.
Repeat. Repeat what you've been listening to so the person feels heard. Also, ask, "Do I have that about right?" Then listen some more.
Move. This is a powerful process to assert leadership. Move your own body, and get other people moving.

One director "Larry" said and did the following. Larry stood up and said, "Stephen (the actor), you stay with me. We'll talk more. John (director of photography), you go huddle with Sarah (assistant director) and get me an estimate of how long it would take to light and prepare set 7 for Scene 41. All of you extras and crew take a 10-minute break off the set. Everyone meet back here at 2:23 pm. Thank you."

You're the leader. Give people direction. Listen. Show that you're paying attention. Show that you face the tough stuff, and give people the impression that they're in good, strong hands.

Points to Remember:

Darkest Secret #4: People will get angry. Deal with it.

Your Countermeasure:
Go neutral, ask questions and listen. Remember to use the process of Breathe, Listen, Repeat, Move.

CHAPTER 5
DARKEST SECRET #5: ON SET, PEOPLE FALL IN AND OUT OF LOVE. OR JUST SLEEP TOGETHER.

On the set of *The Fly* (directed by David Cronenberg), actors Jeff Goldblum and Geena Davis fell in love. This really worked for the film. Goldblum portrayed "Seth," an eccentric, lovable scientist, and Davis portrayed his love interest, "Veronica," a journalist for a science-focused magazine. Seth develops a teleportation device but has an accident: A housefly transports with him but their bodies mingle on a molecular level. I remember the scene when Veronica embraced the oozing and grotesque hybrid-human/fly creature Seth had become. The audience grunted in revulsion. But we all could feel the love between these two people.

That's fine. But what if the couple is arguing on the set? Such arguments can disrupt the production. What happens if the two leads refuse to work together one afternoon? What if there's a tender love scene and the actors are angry with each other?

The blunt truth is that the show goes on. For example, it's reported that Harrison Ford and Sean Young hated each other during the production of *Blade Runner*. What audiences saw as passion was probably only fury. Something similar happened on the set of *An Officer and a Gentleman*. Crew members could not miss the anger between stars Richard Gere and Debra Winger. Again, what seems like passion on the screen was likely anger.

You're the director. People look to you to lead. What do you do?

Don't take sides. You can say something neutral like: "That sounds frustrating" but avoid saying things like, "You're right. He is a thoughtless, stupid jerk. . ."

Agree with the feeling. This means that you agree that the person feels what she feels.

You, as the director, do not need to agree with their assessment of the personality of the other person. Just keep those thoughts to yourself.

Realize a squabble may pass, but you can damage relationships by badmouthing anyone.

The couple may come back together four hours later. But if you've agreed with one of them that the other one is a "stupid jerk" (or worse), together they'll have ammunition against you. And your relationships with both of them will never be the same. My point is you're a director first, and a friend second. Friends listen and empathize. A director listens and leads.

Now, I'll talk about methods for dealing with two tough situations:

a) Your leading man is having an affair with his co-star, but his wife comes for a visit to the set. Do not get into the middle of the situation. Don't get involved in elaborate cover-up schemes. Avoid being the one to tell the wife about the affair. Why? Because you'll likely make an enemy of your leading man, who may say, "Damn you. I was going to tell her myself, at the right time." If the wife asks you about her spouse, reply with something like: "You need to talk to Joe about that."

b) Your co-stars are enraptured with each other and they're coming late to the set every morning. In the morning, film something. Shoot with their stand-ins. Have a high angle shot and show the leading man coming into the scene. Shoot something even if you know that it will likely not be in the finished product. You need to show the studio executives and everyone else that you're getting your shots. Film scenes with other actors with the back of the stand-in in the foreground. When the co-stars finally arrive on set, talk with them privately—and talk with them separately. Do not reprimand people in front of others. Guide each actor to remember why they said yes to the film in the first place. Ask them gentle questions to identify what they value. You can ask something like: "Imagine it's nine months from now, and we all got back to work and did our best. What positive outcomes do you feel you'd be enjoying?"

Points to Remember:

Darkest Secret #5: On set, people fall in and out of love. Or just sleep together.

Your Countermeasure:
Do not take sides. Do not say bad things about the person whom the team member is complaining about.

CHAPTER 6
DARKEST SECRET #6: IF YOU'RE NOT CAREFUL, THE CREW WILL TURN ON YOU.

As a young director, Michael Crichton felt distraught at how things weren't moving as fast as he hoped on the set of his film *The Great Train Robbery*. Why is this trouble? A director can get behind schedule, and a studio can fire said director for going over budget and failing to complete his or her duties.

The assistant director gently suggested that Crichton screen for the crew a previous film Crichton had directed entitled Westworld.

Crichton's problem, according to Crichton's own autobiography, was that he didn't listen to the gentle suggestion of his assistant director. Things were getting out of hand. Finally, Crichton screened his previous film for the crew. Finally, after seeing that film, they became cooperative. Apparently, they were satisfied that the young director knew what he was doing.

One person's craziness is another person's reality. - Tim Burton, director of Batman, Ed Wood, Alice in Wonderland

Actions create lasting impressions. On the set of *The Hunt for Red October*, actor Sean Connery cursed out one hapless production assistant in front of all of the extras (background actors) portraying the sailors under the command of Connery's character. Director John McTiernan later said that he understood what Connery was doing. Connery put all the extras on edge. The extras started to stand taller when Connery walked by. After all he was their captain.

McTiernan thought Connery's actions appropriate. Certainly, they made the film better.

But what works for acting can be a "crash and burn" for the director. If you, as a director, come down that hard on a hapless crew member, the rest of the crew won't respect you. They'll see your actions as abuse.

Things can work up to a crisis. For example, while filming *Titanic*, director James Cameron got into a shouting match with stunt coordinator Simon Crane that escalated to Crane yelling, "Go f—k yourself!" and Cameron replying, "You're fired!" More shouts followed until Crane stormed off the set with sixty stuntpeople following him in a show of solidarity.

Cameron was prepared to let Crane and his people walk. Cameron discussed the situation with producer Jon Landau. Cameron said, "What do you think? Should he be able to say that to me. Say anything you want to me in private. Just don't break the chain of command on the set." But Producer Jon Landau knew that the loss of Crane and sixty stuntpeople would be big trouble with the studio. Some of the stuntmen had already been established as characters. Cameron required a public apology, but Crane balked at that. Fortunately Landau brokered a compromise. Crane apologized to Cameron in front of some department heads, but Crane did not have to apologize in front of his own stuntpeople.

Avoid picking on one person.

I have seen some directors pick one person to "ride" through a production. The better thing is to fire the person if that seems necessary. I have had to fire people, even friends, and the production was better for it. Don't let one person put you in a foul mood and start a negative chain of events that could lead to a crew revolt.

By the first week of shooting, you know exactly where your film is heading based on the psychology of your director. - Jodie Foster, director and actress

To keep the crew from turning on you, do the following:

- Get the crew on your side. Even show your past work so they know your competence.
- Hold the chain of command, and still, if possible, allow people to save face.
- Avoid picking on one person.
- Fire people when necessary.
- Hold your calm. Avoid escalating a situation. Call for a break. Remember from a previous section on dealing with anger on the set: *Breathe. Listen. Repeat. Move* (move yourself and move crew people).

Watch yourself, that is, pay attention to how you're doing. If you feel too prickly, give yourself a break. Perhaps lie down in a trailer for ten minutes. No one cares how you feel. You're the leader. Lead.

It's your job to guide the atmosphere on the set. Many people have reported that Steven Spielberg exudes such glee on the set. He truly enjoys himself and the cast and crew pick up on that. Actor Ben Kingsley said that it feels good when Steven Spielberg exclaims, "That's going to be in the movie!"

Points to Remember:

Darkest Secret #6: If you're not careful, the crew will turn on you.

Your Countermeasure:
Watch yourself. Be careful that you don't "ride" one person on the set. If appropriate, fire that person. Get the crew on your side. Even show your past work so they know your competence. Hold the chain of command, and still, if possible, allow people to save face.

Hold your calm. Avoid escalating a situation. Call for a break if necessary.

CHAPTER 7
DARKEST SECRET #7: SOME PEOPLE WILL DO ANYTHING TO ADVANCE THEMSELVES. A-N-Y-T-H-I-N-G.

A director I know was seduced by a blonde, gymnast actress. Some readers would say, so what's the problem?

Well, she didn't really want him; she wanted a role. What could go wrong? A forlorn director can exude such a bad mood that the crew loses momentum. A director will yell at the AD who will growl at the cinematographer who will chew out a grip. Soon there is chaos. Mistakes happen and the production goes over schedule and over budget. And the director is replaced.

Other situations occur. For example, it's understandable if a director and actor fall into each others' arms during the making of a film because the situation is a bit similar to a battlefield. Intense pressure and struggling for a cause—to complete a good film.

The problem is some people are quick to say that a director's lover is getting preferential treatment. It may be true, but the director and actor can keep their "lovey-dovey" interactions to a minimum in front of the crew. We're not just talking about making a bad impression; we're talking about the morale of the crew. People tend to resent unfairness, and they slow down. The director's job is to demand fast, efficient work. A director loses the crew's respect when it's perceived that inappropriate preferential treatment is occurring.

Some romantic relationships between directors and actors become famous. When Vincente Minnelli directed *Meet Me in St. Louis,* he and Judy Garland didn't get along at all. Then they got along so well that in June 1945 they got married. That's when a relationship turns out okay. But we all know that couples fight. It's counterproductive to have tension on the set. Imagine the disruption if a director's lover gets mad and won't come out of his or her trailer.

Then, complications can ensue if an actress sleeps with the producer who starts interfering with the director's decisions. What can you do? Have a private conversation with the producer. I've had to do it. For one production, I noticed that the producer kept interjecting her own ideas to the actors on the set. I called for a break. In private, I said to the producer, "The actors need to hear one voice—the director's voice. They're getting confused. And that's slowing us down. If you have some concerns, tell me. I'll get things done."

Soon the producer apologized. I did touch a nerve with "that's slowing us down." Producers are concerned with the schedule and the budget.

My point is: be conscious of your behavior in front of the crew. It might also be wise to "go slow" in an attempt to avoid the complications that can ensue from a personal relationship.

In any case, when you're casting and gathering crew for a film, protect your own heart and realize that some people may play your heart like a violin to further their career. You have been warned.

Points to Remember:

Darkest Secret #7: Some people will do anything to advance themselves. A-N-Y-T-H-I-N-G.

Your Countermeasure:
Attempt to "go slow." Stay alert that someone may be cozying up to you to get a role. Perhaps run through your decisions with a counselor or a trusted advisor. And if some romantic relationship on the set is causing problems, talk to the parties separately and in private. Ask them gentle questions to remind them of what they value and why they chose to work on the film in the first place. Get their cooperation and keep up the morale (and speed) of your crew.

CHAPTER 8
DARKEST SECRET #8: GET READY TO BE SCARED.

I could see it on the actress' face. With every line her co-star said, she was getting angrier. I got the feeling of *she's wrecking my movie*. It was all going wrong. She is supposed to be the loving girlfriend trying to support her lover even though he was yelling. His haunting flashbacks of bloodshed and loss of his best friend in a war was twisting him in knots. He was back in the States but really too much of him was lost in the Vietnam war.

As the director, I had to do something quick. The light was going. Soon the day would be done and I would probably lose the chance to shoot this scene properly.

So I whispered in her ear. "I don't believe you. I don't believe you love him. That you're afraid that your relationship is going to end." She glared at me, attempting to fry me with her hatred. But amazingly enough, in the next take she was excellent, tears in her eyes to seize the heart of any audience member.

As a director, you'll witness problem after problem closing in to kill your film.

So what is the fear? That you'll lose it all. The film will turn out horribly, and you'll never get the chance to direct another film.

JAWS was the hardest production I ever experienced. And I still have nightmares about it [thirty five years later].
- Steven Spielberg

Sooner or later, you will know exactly how Spielberg felt. Things will go wrong. Important things. Things you won't have any idea how to make right. Making a film includes at least several moments of sheer, pure, unadulterated terror. Sometimes more. But only if you're doing it right.

There's something I like in everything I've done. But, there's also stuff that I'll look at and all I'll see is the compromise. When I was saying that filmmaking is the art of compromise, when you sit there and all you see is the compromises that were too great that you shouldn't have made. - Gale Anne Hurd, producer of Aliens, The Abyss, Tremors, The Walking Dead TV series

For one of my feature films, I directed a dance sequence. While watching dailies (unedited footage), my heart dropped to the floor. The dailies looked terrible! The set looked horrible. Drab. Bare. With a metal frame stuck in the center of the floor. Who cares that the metal frame was needed for a later scene—when a character would smash a block of wood with a martial arts kick. But in the dance scene, that damn frame looked cheap and laughable.

And we're not done. The actress couldn't dance. With all the weightlifting she engaged in, she walked like a linebacker. The so-called dancing was absolute garbage.

No-no-no! This dance scene was supposed to get our hero to catch his breath. He was supposed to be swept away by the young woman's grace and sensual appeal. Forget it! It was not there!

What could I do? Save the scene in the editing room—hopefully. What did Spielberg do with a mechanical shark that wouldn't work? He hinted at the shark. I decided to do that with this dance. I'd spend more time on the hero, watching her. His face would tell the story. And for her, I'd use close ups. No laughable, dreary wide shots. I drew up more storyboards and we reshot the scene the next day.

How to Cope With the Fear

1. Realize that filmmakers simply get disappointed and scared when watching dailies.

I got better at dealing with watching dailies when I told myself: "Yes, I'll get disappointed. But I can fix this somehow."

2. Watch other films and note how other directors have solved problems.

Steven Spielberg said that when the mechanical shark of *Jaws* didn't work, he thought about how Alfred Hitchcock would have shot the film. That one idea led to a number of ideas to imply the presence of the shark.

3. Pull your trusted team members close.

Spielberg had a "secret weapon" for dealing with the troubles of making *Jaws:* the editor Verna Fields, known as "mother cutter." She grabbed bits of film from disparate scenes and made something cohesive. When she did not have the ideal shot, she created the impression of the shark by pulling together various shots. Ask your department heads for ideas.

A highlight of *Jaws* is when Quint (portrayed by Robert Shaw) tells a gripping tale of 1100 men going into the water as the Indianapolis sank and how the sharks dined on so many that only 300 men were rescued. When I say "pull your trusted team members close," I invite you to look at how many people worked on that scene. Playwright Howard Sackler conceived the scene. Then Spielberg's friend screenwriter John Milius lengthened the scene, and actor Robert Shaw rewrote it. Co-star Roy Scheider contributed "doll's eyes" to the speech: "And the thing about a shark is he's got lifeless eyes. Black eyes. Like a doll's eyes."

You're not alone when things go wrong. Ask for assistance.

4. Realize you can solve a problem often by revising the script.

For one of my films, the screenplay had the cute meet (first time the romantic leads meet) on a bus. I knew the budget was stretched. A bus required permits, twelve extras, off-duty police officers, and a designated area of street for filming. So I changed the script—from "interior bus" to "interior elevator." I said, "Let's build an elevator set in the living room of the apartment we're renting for the production." No permits, four extras including my then girlfriend, no off-duty police officers. I saved the budget and the scene turned out better than my first idea of the bus. Later, people marveled at how "Anne" managed to say her name just before the elevator doors closed. Well, of course.

The elevator doors were hand operated!

Training for *Rocky III*, Sylvester Stallone tore a muscle in his chest so that he could not punch with his left hand. A boxing movie and the star can't use his left arm? And Rocky is a southpaw (left-handed boxer). So a director-writer stews for a while—until creativity brings a solution. Stallone changed the script so that he didn't punch with his left hand to confuse his opponent Clubber Lang. Later, Stallone said, "It improved the film."

5. "Protect the talent."

No matter what happens, remember these three words: "Protect the talent." Don't let your concern about technical matters spill onto your actors. You think you have problems—okay—but don't add to them with scared cast and crew members.

The magic doesn't come from within the director's mind, it comes from within the hearts of the actors. - James Cameron

The whole cast and crew trust you to lead them through the forest. By the way, find someone, perhaps a trusted friend or counselor, outside of the production to talk with on the phone at least. Don't treat anyone on the set as your "confessor." While making *Jaws*, Steven Spielberg got on the phone and talked with his film industry friends George Lucas, Martin Scorsese and writer-director John Milius to unload his woes.

I remember a line spoken by Dr. McCoy of the original *Star Trek* series, "Let your people do their jobs, Jim." So yes, you'll need to have faith in yourself and you'll ask for assistance, but you won't burden people with your occasional, inevitable doubts.

6. Think of David Mamet's suggestion, "A traditional recipe for genius: inspiration, a plan, not enough time."

Go back to the original inspiration for your film. What drew you to the project in the first place?

I think there's only one or two films where I've had all the financial support I needed. All the rest, I wish I'd had the money to shoot another ten days.- Martin Scorsese, director of GoodFellas, The Aviator

Scorsese commands sizable budgets, but he feels the crunch, too. So what do you do? Dive in. Make the hard decisions. Cut scenes. Combine scenes. Draw up ten possible ways to do things. And go to your department heads and say, "I need some solutions here. Come up with at least three ideas. Endorse one and tell me your reasons for that one."

I think that's the key to being a director: to be able to get the shot and move on quickly.
Bobby Farrelly, co-director of There's Something About Mary; Dumb and Dumber

7. Remember the battles that went into the production of great films.

Every day of production of *The Godfather* (directed by Francis Ford Coppola) and *Jaws* (directed by Steven Spielberg), the young directors faced the possibility of being fired.

A number of classic films ran low on funds. For example, for *Rocky*, Stallone had to rewrite the first date scene between Rocky and his girlfriend Adrian to take place in a closed ice rink because the production did not have the funds for thirty extras. The scene turned out much better! It's one of my favorite scenes of all time. It's quirky. Adrian barely skates while Rocky runs on the ice next to her. And the two characters reveal endearing and humble details about their thoughts and lives. Excellent!

Coping with fear is a combination of having a strong mindset (informed by the above seven methods) and gathering your resources.

Points to Remember:

Darkest Secret #8: Get ready to be scared.

Your Countermeasure:
Have someone, perhaps a counselor or trusted friend not part of the production, to talk with—at least by phone. Do not unburden your heart to cast or crew members because they're relying on you to maintain composure and lead them through the forest. Use these methods:

1. Realize that filmmakers simply get disappointed and scared when watching dailies.
2. Watch other films and note how directors have solved problems.
3. Pull your trusted team members close.
4. Realize you can solve a problem often by revising the script.
5. "Protect the talent."
6. Think of David Mamet's suggestion: "A traditional recipe for genius: inspiration, a plan, not enough time."
7. Remember the battles that went into the production of great films.

Tom Marcoux

CHAPTER 9
DARKEST SECRET #9: THE EDITING ROOM CAN MAKE YOU FEEL STUPID AND HOW TO AVOID THAT

Listen closely: What feels right on the set often shows up as "deadwood" in the editing room. Why?

a) When scenes are cut together, some elements now appear repetitious (or as "overkill").

b) The pacing has slowed down.

c) Some dialogue feels "forced."

d) Some detail can be expressed economically.

A skilled actor can use a stern look that can convey a lot. You don't need a bunch of words like: "Shut up. Now is not the time to talk about that! Not with these people here."

The issue here is to provide yourself with "cutting room"—the ability to modify scenes when you're in the editing room.

Recently, I read a book by film writer-director David Mamet (screenwriter of *The Untouchables* starring Sean Connery and Kevin Costner) in which he described two solutions he learned from John Sayles (writer-director of *Lone Star*):

Solution 1: Film the character walking in and sitting down for the beginning of a scene. Then also, film the character walking out of the scene and exiting.

Solution 2: Film the character looking up, then down, then right and left. [You can use the head and eye movements to "motivate a cut."]

"Motivate a cut" is an editing term that relates to placing shots in sequence in a seamless manner. So if the actor looks right and the next shot matches the action by showing a car zooming left to right, the editor has "motivated the cut."

Another Solution: Get "coverage."
This is the process of filming close-ups, over the shoulder shots, two-shots and a master shot (a view of the whole scene). Over the shoulder shots provide you with the chance to change dialogue (since you cannot see one character's lips).

I tend to film a two-shot first so that I'm close to the actors and can pick up their first efforts. Sometimes one catches lightning in a bottle. And I do not want to waste the actor's first and perhaps best take on a master shot. Along these lines, Steven Spielberg says that he films the rehearsal.

As you work with each scene, make sure that you use the above solutions so you can improve your film during postproduction.

Points to Remember:

Darkest Secret #9: The Editing Room Can Make You Feel Stupid and How to Avoid That

Your Countermeasure:

Be sure to film the character walking in and sitting down at the beginning of a scene. Also, film the character looking up, then down, then right and left. These techniques provides you with options in the editing room. Finally, be sure to get "coverage."

CHAPTER 10
DARKEST SECRET #10: EVERYBODY HAS TUNNEL VISION. INCLUDING YOU.

Movies are like an expensive form of therapy for me.
- Tim Burton, director of Ed Wood *and* Edward Scissorhands

On the set of *Saturday Night Fever*, star John Travolta absolutely refused to play the scene in the manner director John Badham requested. Travolta felt that his character would never crouch on a beam that was attached to the Verrazano Narrows Bridge (which connects Brooklyn with Staten Island). It was a dangerous stunt requiring a stuntman to crouch and hug a beam hundreds of feet above the water.

Travolta's tunnel vision focused on his character. Badham's tunnel vision involved making the shots match. How could he finish the film if Travolta's standing but the stuntman's crouching do not match? In the final cut of the film, you can see the crouching stuntman in a shot. It never matched.

Tunnel vision is often defined as "vision in which the visual field is severely constricted, as from within a tunnel looking out (*American Heritage Dictionary*)" and . . . "narrowness of viewpoint resulting from concentration on a single idea, opinion, etc., to the exclusion of others (*Collins English Dictionary*)."

Why do people develop tunnel vision? Because they are concentrating on their job. Pretty much nothing else. You want them to concentrate that way. Until it turns into a brick wall.

The actor is concerned with his own bit of it, but the director's somehow trying to work the whole thing into a much bigger picture. It's like conducting an orchestra. - Roland Joffe, director of The Mission *and* The Killing Fields

For example, I was directing a feature film and the actor portraying "Mark" just couldn't find that way to say a line. Mark was telling his friend about how, if he just swerved his car, he would have prevented a head-on collision that killed his wife.

The actor couldn't find a way to say, "I just had to swerve . . . Debbie."

What did I do? I filmed the first takes with the actor doing it his way. Was it worth getting into a tussle with the actor over this one line? Probably not. I could compensate for that line in postproduction if necessary. How? I could add a line to another scene. Perhaps, one character confides to another: "Eventually, Mark managed to tell me about the accident. He was high on something and could not swerve in time to prevent the accident. His wife died, and . . . "

And if it really became critical, I could use ADR (automatic dialogue replacement) to put the lines in while the camera is on the other character. I might show a cut of the scene to the actor and talk about a problem the audience was having with the scene.

Your job as director is to see that there are many options. You need to be flexible. You're there to tell the story as best as you can. You need to get past tunnel vision.

You're telling the story through external things, which is what directing is. Directing is turning psychology into behavior. - Elia Kazan, director of On the Waterfront *and* A Streetcar Named Desire

So if an actor is stuck or stubborn, write down a list of 10 ways you can work around the situation. You'll probably gain cooperation when you show that you value the contributions of your actors. If they have an unusual idea, give them a take that is "their way." You can say, "Sounds interesting. Let's try that."

Some directors make the mistake of talking too much to certain actors. Often, you don't have to tell the actor that something is not working. Let the actor try a take and discover that something is off.

I do think that's so much a part of what being a director is—in working with actors—to really try and be sensitive to what each actor needs to get to where he wants to be.
Bill Condon, director of Dreamgirls and Kinsey

By the way, to keep the atmosphere positive on the set, express your appreciation. Thank people. Make sure you express your appreciation for the person's talent, skill and effort. To do that, you'll need to expand your vision beyond just getting your shots.

People have long memories. Express your appreciation to the person and in front of others. Director Frank Capra failed to express appreciation to his screenwriter Robert Riskin when Capra was interviewed for an article. Instead, Capra talked about his techniques on the set that comprise "The Capra Touch." Later, Riskin gave Capra a new script—but it was made of blank pages. Riskin had a note attached: "Dear Frank, put 'the Capra touch' on this!"

As the director, keep your focus on getting your shots, and make sure that you expand your vision so that you can come with a lot of options for times when you deal with cast or crew members' tunnel vision.

Points to Remember:

Darkest Secret #10: Everybody has tunnel vision. Including you.

Your Countermeasure:

If you're confronted with a cast or crew member who is stuck, let the person try a take and see what happens. Instead of just telling people things are not working, see if you can let them experience the situation. Come up with ten options when there is a bumpy situation. You, as the director, need both your pinpoint focus and peripheral vision.

CHAPTER 11
DARKEST SECRET #11: YOU DON'T SAVE TIME BY BEING ABRUPT. YOU MAKE PEOPLE ANGRY. INSTEAD LISTEN AND TREAT EACH PERSON ACCORDING TO THEIR UNIQUE QUALITIES.

Now more than ever we need to talk to each other, to listen to each other and understand how we see the world, and cinema is the best medium for doing this. - Martin Scorsese, director of Raging Bull *and* Casino

Ever sent an email and received a reply that blindsided you? One in which the recipient was furious and you had no notion why? If so, you can see that either sender or receiver can make an error.

Let's face it. People interpret things often by their "internal weather" and not by what's outside. So how do you avoid needless conflict? Listen to the person first.

Listening first is the ideal. But sometimes, you'll need people to move fast. For example, "magic time" occurs when the sun is setting and turning the sky golden. You only have five minutes to get a shot. With the daylight fading, you can say, "Yes. I want to listen to what you're talking about. How about we get this shot. We only have five minutes of magic time left. Then, we'll sit down and talk about that."

To avoid being abrupt, I often end a phone conversation or even a brief meeting in person with questions like:
- "Is there anything else I need to know?"
- "Do you have any questions for me?"
- "Are things okay?"

I like to nip troubles in the bud. That means, I need to listen and hear people out.

Among my friends, I find two people in particular who like to be abrupt and "solve" things with one quick email. Probably that starts a flame war. One email began with two words: "ENOUGH ALREADY!" Yes, I know: all capital letters means shouting in email. So that email raised tempers and some friends will not attend parties at the email sender's home. Both of these guys (you knew they were guys, right?) think they're saving time. But we then spend so much more time unraveling the mess. I call what they do a "false saving of time."

Another example. On the set of *Three Kings*, actor George Clooney said to director David O. Russell, "David, it's a big [tough] day. But you can't shove, push or humiliate people who aren't allowed to defend themselves." According to Clooney, Russell had been verbally and physically demeaning the crew. As a newspaper reported, Russell didn't take this well: "Why don't you just worry about your [expletive removed] acting?! You're being a [expletive removed]. You want to hit me? You want to hit me? Come on, [expletive removed], hit me!"

Russell grabbed Clooney by the throat. Clooney then punched the director. That was in 1999; Clooney still says that he'll never work with Russell again.

When something like a fight happens on the set or if cast or crew people storm off, the production comes to a stop. The director gets behind schedule, goes over budget, and makes himself vulnerable to being fired.

My point is that a director is called upon to be extraordinarily patient. And smart directors push themselves to avoid being abrupt with team members. It works much better when a director listens and treats each person according to their unique qualities. For example, Anthony Hopkins does not want to talk much about the script. He studies the script and steps in front of the camera. Other actors want to "delve deeply" into the script. The wise director pays close attention and helps actors feel supported in the way they prefer to feel supported. This reminds me of "Platinum Rule" (originated by Dr. Tony Alessandra and Michael O'Connor): "Do unto others as they want done unto them."

Points to Remember:

Darkest Secret #11: You don't save time by being abrupt. You make people angry. Instead listen and treat each person according to their unique qualities.

Your Countermeasure:

Catch yourself when you find that you want to say something abruptly. Pause. Take a breath. Ask a gentle question to the person you're talking with and listen. [Yes, there are situations when being abrupt may be the appropriate response. For example, if someone's safety is at risk, a loud "No!" may be the best reaction.]

CHAPTER 12
DARKEST SECRET #12: NO MATTER WHAT YOU DO, SOME PEOPLE WILL NEVER UNDERSTAND.

People told me I couldn't kill [Jack] Nicholson, so I cast him in two roles and killed him off twice. - Tim Burton, director of Ed Wood *and* Edward Scissorhands

For one feature film I directed, I asked the lead actress to come in to record new lines (a process called Automatic Dialogue Replacement). She refused and said, "I know what happens. My acting teacher told me. I'll lose my close-ups."

So I made several attempts to explain the importance of improving the film with the new lines. I talked about how her close-ups did not matter if the film did not make sense. Nothing I said worked. She continued to refuse.

So what could I do? I replaced her voice through the whole feature film.

My biggest role as director on the film is keeping a sense of the overview—how to cast the movie and shoot it in such a way that it will cut together. And how to design the style and tone.

- Jay Roach (director of Meet the Parents *and* Austin Powers: International Man of Mystery*)*

No matter what you do, some people will never understand what you're saying, what your intentions are, and what you're doing. It's a fact that some people don't 'get' what you're trying to say and you mustn't let that drive you crazy. Some people will totally misinterpret your actions on set. Some will go off on a tangent, unable to grasp the vision you have even though they are working on the same film.

What can you do then? First, you make sure that you do not escalate the situation by yelling or badmouthing people.

Second, even if people won't be agreeable, you must still demonstrate that you are confident in your own vision. The idea is to request what you want. Express your reasoning.

The point of having a director is that they make the final decision; it's their point of view, they set the rhythm and they make the final decisions. - Christian Bale

Elsewhere in this book, we covered "be a director first, a friend second." Let's face it. You can't be friends with everyone. The most important thing is to do your job in a professional and cordial manner. How can you do right by people? Make the film as best you can.

At the same time, you're the leader. Leaders feel lonely sometimes. For example, I completed an audio program that none of my closest friends like. I had to go with my gut feeling that a small niche target audience exists for the audio program. My friends do not like the audio program; that is okay. It is not for them. Much of the value of the program, which I funded personally through my own company, is that I finished the project, learned a lot doing it, and the performers and crew got paid.

A leader does what needs to be done and stands tall even when some people disagree fervently.

How do you stand tall?

Write down why you're doing the project. I've talked with other directors who have these goals and thoughts for a project:

- This is an important story to bring to people's awareness.
- This will demonstrate what I can do.
- This project will further the careers of those involved.
- My heart tells me that this is a film that I need to do.

Identify why you want to do something and you can withstand the times when "how" is tough.

Points to Remember:

Darkest Secret #12: No matter what you do, some people will never understand.

Your Countermeasure:

Identify your goals for a project. Focus on why you want to do, realizing that sometimes, certain people will never understand your intentions no matter what you do. As the leader, you must stand tall, radiate confidence, and guide people forward.

CHAPTER 13
DARKEST SECRET #13: YOUR CLOSEST FRIEND ON SET WILL FAIL YOU.

You hope and pray that you'll get involved with a director that you understand and who has the same sensibility as you do and knows how to push you and bring out the best in you.
- Matthew Modine, actor

So your job includes pushing people. That includes pushing your closest friend on set. What happens? Your friend will probably resent it at some point. What do people do with resentment? Some talk it out. Others start "acting out." Someone might forget an important detail which could ruin an afternoon of filming. For example, the filming schedule for *Rocky* was twenty-seven days. One lost day could torpedo the film. In fact, the crew did sixty camera setups in one day. The average is twenty.

Let's face it: human beings make mistakes. It just seems to hurt more when a friend does it. So a friend may make a mistake not from resentment but from "being upside down" in his own life. I have some friends who seem to be "walking panic." They are people I will talk with a bit at a gathering, but I would not hire them. Filmmaking is stressful and I need the most alert and competent and trustworthy people, not the nicest or most entertaining.

A good director creates an environment, which gives the actor the encouragement to fly. - Kevin Bacon

Bacon is talking about an ideal for directors to aim for. How about the days when you're exhausted? Who will support you then? It's important to develop a support system (outside of your filmmaking team) that helps you stay strong and healthy. Why is this important? Because it's your job to guide people and to get them to pull their weight if they're slipping up. And that includes your closest friend on set. In fact, it's crucial because it hurts more when a friend is letting you down!

A support system can include things you do to take care of yourself and perhaps, a confidante. Football player Rosie Grier knitted. Robert DeNiro would get up at 4 AM to work out before a filming day. You need a support system to take care of yourself whether it is a hobby or exercise. For example, Trey Parker, co-creator of TV series *South Park* and of the musical *The Book of Mormon*, tinkers with Lego kits. He says, "It gives me a chance to use my brain in a different way." I also build Lego kits. A student brought Lego to my attention when she gave a speech in my graduate level public speaking class. On especially hectic days, I sometimes take a break to listen to music and tinker with my Lego. Lego is part of my support system. I also make sure to laugh every day by watching something funny on YouTube.com (often standup comedy) or something I recorded on my digital video recorder. I often watch the improvisational comedy show *Whose Line Is It, Anyway?*

Who can you talk with (not related to a film project) and decompress? You might consider talking with a counselor before you have a difficult conversation with your closest friend on the set. Why? Because you want to do a process called "letting go marbles." Author and stress management expert Roger Mellot used marbles as a metaphor for bad things, things we metaphorically swallow. We spend the day swallowing "marbles," feel sick and then inappropriately spew the marbles.

Instead, Mellot urges us to "release the marbles" by talking with a counselor or, perhaps, writing things on paper. (Be sure to tear up the paper and not reread it. Otherwise, you "re-swallow those same marbles.")

Walt Disney had a way to release marbles. At the end of each workday, he would talk with his personal nurse Hazel George as she massaged his neck.

You may hesitate to devote money to a counselor, nurse, or personal trainer, but let's notice that Steven Spielberg hired personal trainer, Jake Steinfeld, to accompany him on the set of *Indiana Jones and the Temple of Doom*. Spielberg believes in keeping up his physical health. Steinfeld also trained Harrison Ford both before and during the production of the same film. Research backs up the notion that physical training also provides mental health benefits.

So far, we've covered the ideas that you need to take care of yourself through exercise, a hobby, other facets of a support system, "releasing marbles," a personal trainer, and perhaps, a counselor. Why? Because you need to be able to address problems during production of your film. We already noted that when a friend slips up it can hurt your feelings more. Because you may be thinking, "He's my friend. He should be trying to help me here. He should not be putting me at risk!"

Here are other vital topics related to a close friend failing you.

Danger signs to look for.

Is your friend flaunting any standards of professional behavior? Is he chronically late to the set? Does he goof off in some way? Does he hide and let other people do the heavy lifting (if his job calls for that)? Does he flaunt his status as your friend? Does he take liberties and brag about being your friend? Is he slipping deadlines and holding you up?

What to talk with a counselor about.

Talking with a counselor is helpful for you to say aloud all your concerns about the danger signs. You'll probably want to confirm whether you're making too big a thing about anything that you're observing. And you can rehearse with the counselor how you will talk with your friend who is failing you.

How to warn a friend he's slipping up.

You want to find your own personal way of saying the tough things. Perhaps you can say something like:

"It's really tough for me to say this. But you're my good friend, and I need to tell you the truth. I really need something different from you—from someone who's doing [the job] for this film. So do you want to hear what kind of help I need here?"

You'll notice that I've included a question. Research shows that people are quite concerned about their own autonomy. If someone just gives them a "lecture," they tend to emotionally shut down.

Instead, use the method of "ask for permission"—to get the person to feel that they have some authority over themselves. So when you ask a question like: "So this is a good time for us to talk about some tough stuff now?"—and you get a 'yes' answer—then your friend feels some autonomy. If your friend replies, "No," you can respond, "Okay. We need to talk about this today. How about 2 PM or 7 PM?"

Let's face it. You're the boss. But some bosses are better at being respectful. Just issuing orders does not insure good morale on the set. You can still be firm and say things in a cordial manner as you provide direction.

Reconcile friendship with your job of getting the film done.

After you've warned your friend about actions that need to done or bad habits that need to stop, observe if he makes any improvements.

If no improvements occur and you try again to get your point across, then you may find that you need to fire your friend. You need to find your own personal way to discuss the situation. Rehearsing with a counselor can help. Here is an example of one (among many) ways to talk about the ending of the job:

"Nick, you're important to me. You're my good friend since 2000 and I'm hoping for years beyond this film. And I've got a job here. I can't let this film sink like a ship. I cannot make mistakes that could get me fired. Look, it seems like we don't have a fit between you, your job and what I need here. So let's end the job here. We'll call it creative differences."

This is only a sound bite of a whole conversation. You'll need to work out your own way of talking about the tough situation. That's why I have repeatedly mentioned working with a counselor or trusted advisor. And rehearsing.

And sometimes, you'll lose the friend. One of the friends I fired left my life. It wasn't explosive. He just drifted away, and I'm not looking him up on Facebook. Another friend I fired is still my friend. We get together socially every month. Some friendships go on a long time, metaphorically like a novel. Other friendships are short stories. We do the best we can.

In summary, your closest friend will make a mistake and it will hurt more. It's best that you take care of yourself and "release the marbles" before you confront the person.

Points to Remember:

Darkest Secret #13: Your closest friend on set will fail you.

Your Countermeasure:
Take care of yourself and "release the marbles" before you confront the person. Remember to use a whole support system that may include (but not be limited to): exercise, a hobby, a personal trainer, and perhaps, a counselor.

CHAPTER 14
DARKEST SECRET #14: PREPARE TO HAVE TO FIRE SOMEONE.

In a movie, you're raw material, just a hue of some color and the director makes the painting. - Viggo Mortensen, lead actor in The Lord of the Rings

Some people report that Steven Spielberg has his associates fire people. That way he retains his reputation as a nice guy.

I've had to fire friends. In the years since that time, I'm more careful about hiring people in the first place.

I have had to end projects. Back in college, I gave back $20,000 and ended production of a music album. One person connected to the investors was trying to take over, and I could sense the project would spiral downwards. To end the project, I had to cover $1,000 that a friend had already spent on a synthesizer. And I had to cover my own $1,000 advance; this was tough because I was barely holding things together as I worked my way through college.

I once read: "The time to fire someone is the first time you think of it." Well, that idea sounds extreme, and it may not always apply. But it does get me thinking about situations in which we might wait too long to get a disruptive person off our set. If someone is slacking, it really bothers other team members. Why? They're doing their best and it simply feels unfair that someone else can coast. This situation can also create a cascade of "de-motivation." For example, one chronically late person may encourage others to be late. The damage continues.. Do not let that happen. Face the situation. Rehearse the words you will use when firing the person. Perhaps rehearse in front of a trusted advisor. Get some legal advice if necessary.

Perhaps you pride yourself on being a nice person. When you took on the job of director, you stepped into the part of leader. Now, getting things done through people is more important than "being nice." However, you can tell yourself that firing someone may be a benefit not only to you and the team, but also to the fired person. How? When you fire someone, "you free up their future." Many times, people have a bad fit, but they will not quit on their own. Help them get on with their life. And just as important, free yourself of the energy drain of someone pulling down the production.

Realize this: if you have one slacker, you're teaching other team members that it's okay to be a slacker on the production. Stop that. Make sure that everyone pulls his or her weight. And you'll keep up the morale on your set.

Up to this point, we've covered the importance of firing a "slacker." Here are other topics related to firing someone.

Pay attention to subtle causes for firing someone.

It's obvious that one needs to fire the guy who's never on time. It's different if you have a nice script supervisor who never repeats a mistake but every few days makes a new one. This takes me back to the idea: "People may have a bad fit, but they will not quit on their own. Help them get on with their life." Someone may be a poor script supervisor but an excellent scenery painter.

Some considerations for what you say when firing someone

For many people, it is best to write down your reasons and go over them with a trusted advisor, perhaps legal counsel. Why? According to a study in *The Economic Journal*, Americans spend more money on civil litigation than any other industrialized country, and twice as much on litigation as on the amounts they pay for new cars. Further, the American Bar Association notes that since 2006, over 1 million lawyers are practicing law in the United States. That's more per capita than any other country.

Why the statistics? Simply, there are many lawyers willing to take the case if someone wants to claim a wrongful termination of employment.

So that situation has consequences. If you have an actor (for example) who wants you to fire a crew member, tread carefully. Be sure to document the crew member's lapses in performance. It may be important to get statements of witnesses. You'll also want to document your warnings and conversations with the crew member in your good faith attempts to get him to improve his performance of job duties.

You can summarize your efforts, the continued poor performance, comments about said poor performance from other team members in a letter. Have appropriate personnel (like the producer and legal counsel) sign off on the letter. Then when you call in the team member to the job termination meeting, state things simply. Some management consultants suggest that one has a witness in the room. The producer would be a good witness. Further, management consultants suggest that one says something like: "Myrtle, we need to end your work with the production. The reasons are summarized in this letter which I will give you in a moment. After my meetings with you, we did not see improvements in your performance—which is documented in this letter. We expect that this job termination is not a complete surprise to you. Good luck." At this point, you're standing and you hand the letter to the person. Say nothing more. Do not express your own doubts of your communications because that might provide fuel for Myrtle and a potential lawyer.

The film is your ship. You are charged with, metaphorically, getting everyone safely to your destination—a film completed with quality. As the leader, you must prepare yourself for the tough duties. Firing someone is one of them.

Points to Remember:

Darkest Secret #14: Prepare to have to fire someone.

Your Countermeasure:
Identify who you need to fire and fire them sooner rather than later. Rehearse what you need to say with a trusted advisor. Consider having the producer as your witness and having documented poor performance in a letter for the team member. Get legal advice if appropriate.

CHAPTER 15
DARKEST SECRET #15: STYLE IS NOT ENOUGH. BUT YOU STILL NEED IT.

There were movies that always made me want to be a director. You see brilliant scenes and the way the emotions were handled. I thought, I'd really like to do that. - Bruce Beresford (director of Driving Miss Daisy *and* Tender Mercies*)*

You have a filmmaking style even on your first film. Really? Yes—it's likely made of the film moments you have treasured from films you've enjoyed during your lifetime. You'll make certain decisions based on what you like. People in the industry will view the finished film and the results of your decisions will be considered "your style."

For example, for one film, I made two particular decisions that had an emotional impact. I decided that the camera would be a bit lower for each shot with the two buddies. In this way they would feel a bit heroic. This bothered my primary cameraman because he was tall! He had to set up the camera and then lean over to look through the viewfinder. He grumbled quietly, and sometimes, I had to remind him to lower the camera.

Another decision was to have the leading lady always wear something red in every scene. Why? I wanted to get both the feeling of warmth and passion—and also a volatile energy. This worked as good foreshadowing because she emotionally bubbles over at the end of the film. Such decisions made up the style of my film.

My point is you need to make definitive decisions. Lead the film in your own way. That becomes your style.

Style can include:
- the look
- the sound design (realistic or operatic for example)
- pace of dialogue / amount of dialogue / vocabulary
- emphasis on production design [a studied emphasis on architecture, wardrobe and more]
- unity

One of the important things a director brings to a film is "unity" which can be defined as "A principle of art [that] occurs when all of the elements of a piece combine to make a balanced, harmonious, complete whole (Shelley Esaak, About.com Guide)."

Unity is a crucial element that helps a director provide a satisfying experience for the audience. Often, an audience member reflects on a film and realizes that everything about the film led inevitably to the ending. That is a mark of unity. Author John Howard Lawson, in his book on screenwriting, wrote that unity comes from the climax. I agree. When I write a screenplay, I know early on what my ending is so I can sprinkle the details that push the screenplay forward to that climax—that ending.

As you follow the escapades or the journey of the hero through a story, it evokes some kind of emotion in the viewers. The director's job is to make sure that the audience goes through the journey and has an emotional reaction. - Don Bluth, director of The Secret of Nimh *and* Anastasia

Style creates emotion in the viewer. I'll add that style is not enough. The film may look gorgeous but if you and I don't care about the character—so what? If the story is not fascinating, who cares about the film? For example, I recently saw the film *Sherlock Holmes* starring Robert Downey, Jr. and Jude Law. The first forty minutes held my attention. But somewhere in the second act of the film, I started tinkering with a puzzle. Why? Elements of the film had descended into cliché. Like cookie cutter patterns, a bunch of officials were about to be murdered, while a huge henchmen guarded the death device whose activation counted down. (Anyone remember Oddjob from the James Bond film *Goldfinger*?) Then, the final confrontation between antagonist and protagonist, with the former dying by falling from a great height (just as countless other villains in films from *Batman* to *Die Hard*).

It's tough to keep on throwing fresh details into the latter part of a film. Along those lines, I found Josh Whedon's film *Serenity* to work well.

One pattern he used was
- Oh no!
- Now what?
- Oh, yes!

He had . . . **Spoiler Alert** . . . beloved character Hoban "Wash" Washburne killed.

Whedon said that he did that so that the audience would

feel "anything can happen!"

That is the "Oh, no!" factor.

Two more characters are struck down, wounded, leaving one lone, thin teenage girl River Tam to stand up to about twenty Reavers (crazed, super strong, mutated humans). She jumps into a room with them and starts kicking and hacking at them with bladed weapons. Moments later, the doors are open and she is the lone one standing. She defeated them all. And the audience cheered. It was an "Oh, yes!" moment.

As a side note: we knew that River had been modified and programmed by the government. We just didn't know her special abilities were that powerful.

Now, some readers may protest that the above example of *Serenity* is about writing. I understand, but this is my opportunity to say that the director is "the leader of the screenplay." What I mean is that often directors go back to the screenwriter and request that certain elements be heightened. Directors in American cinema have a lot of input on screenplays.

My point is the great characters and compelling storytelling need to combine with style.

Points to Remember:

Darkest Secret #15: Style is not enough. But you still need it.

Your Countermeasure:

Identify your style and be sure it serves the story of the film. Realize that style cannot make up the hole left by no great characters and no compelling storytelling. Lead the screenwriter to provide what you need in terms of storytelling.

CHAPTER 16
DARKEST SECRET #16: SOONER OR LATER, YOU WILL SECOND-GUESS YOURSELF.

It's coming. What? That moment when you feel paralyzing self-doubt: A moment feeling overwhelmed or the loss of focus that robs a director of the vision she needs to do her job. There will be a time when it appears that no one agrees with you.

What can you do? Prepare! Start with a notebook of your original intentions. Director Elia Kazan suggested that you have notes of your original intentions with every scene of the film.

One of the important things that a director does is provide unity for the film. As I mentioned earlier unity occurs "when all of the elements of a piece combine to make a balanced, harmonious, complete whole." A good film flows in such a way that the ending appears, upon reflection, inevitable. Author John Howard Lawson, in his book *Theory and Technique of Playwriting and Screenwriting* wrote that unity comes from the climax. So what do we do with that unity-climax idea? Identify how the hero is different at the end of the film. What has she learned? What did she have to go through so she could (at the end) dig deep and find that inner well of courage, hidden talent and natural brilliance? Don't just think about this in a vague way, write down your notes. Because you will refer to your notes when you're second guessing yourself.

Continue with writing more notes about:

1) how your film has unity derived from the climax. (Make sure that your character has a "character arc"—that means, she starts as "less" and ends up as "more." More resourceful or even does something courageous for the first time.)

2) the main character to help guide your casting decisions.

3) your original intentions for the film (How do you want the audience to feel? What new thoughts do you want to inspire in your audience?)

3) your original intentions with every scene.

Often, directors second-guess themselves out of a concern for being fresh and original. Julia Cameron, author of *The Artist's Way*, wrote that "original" means that you're the origin of the work. I have always found comfort in that comment. Because then I don't have to put too much focus on "being original." I'm a unique individual; of course, I'll put idiosyncrasies into my work. My work expresses part of me. Just as your work naturally expresses part of you.

By the way, each film or book that I create is merely a snapshot of what I thought and felt at one moment of time. I don't think of it as "representing me." This gives me the freedom to explore and expand my efforts. And to take appropriate risks. On the other hand, fear would make me hesitate and perhaps, go for the cliché and safe decisions.

So what do you do about second guessing yourself? Allow it to exist. By this, I mean let yourself be human and work through it. How? You keep going and exploring. You take a good look at how you're making your decisions. And here is something that's important. You learn to dig deeper in yourself: Ask yourself—am I making decisions based on fear or intuition?

Here is a fast way to assess how you're making decisions:
- Fear invites you to contract, hide, take safe routes.
- Intuition invites you to expand, explore, experiment, take appropriate risks.

So when you second-guess yourself, look at your notebook for your original intentions and your thoughts on unity. Now submit your conflicting thoughts to the "fear or intuition" test (see the contrasting details above).

Every film is a risk. Each production brings up fears. Your task as a director is to lead yourself first. Don't allow yourself to wander around in your thinking. Use the tool of the consummate artist: Get down to specifics.

Here's an example. In recent years, many comedic films have at least one "gross-out" or "way-over-the-top" scene. Let's say that Sarah has second thoughts about including a "gross-out" moment. Here are her thoughts:
- What if I'm going too far?
- What if I lose the audience's empathy for the Miranda character?
- What if I disgust my parents? My hometown. Every well-educated person in America? In the whole world?
- What if I get stuck in making stupid gross-out

comedies for my whole career?
- What if I shoot the damn scene and it gets cut and I wasted all that time and money? And the producer badmouths me and I can't get opportunities to direct ever again?

Where are these questions coming from? Fear.

Now, Sarah turns this around to focus on accessing intuition (the place of "expand, explore, experiment, take appropriate risks").

She has this mix of questions and thoughts that are aligned with intuition and expansion:
- How about I'm going far enough? I'm shaking up the audience and the scene is unpredictable and fresh!
- Maybe this is exactly what will get the audience on Miranda's side. She's confused, upset and so human!
- My parents wouldn't see this kind of film, anyway.
- I'm jumping ahead of myself. The job is make this one film the best I (and my team) can. Stop thinking about imaginary next movies!
- Lots of films cut scenes. It's part of the process. Look, James Cameron cut a chase scene that cost $1 million dollars to film from the final cut of *Titanic*. That was the right decision. That's what directors do.
- I cannot know exactly how I'll feel in the editing room. My job now is to get enough good, fresh, interesting material.
- This scene just feels right to me.

Take the time to think through and feel through your decisions. Assess how you're making decisions from either fear or intuition.

Points to Remember:

Darkest Secret #16: Sooner or later, you will second-guess yourself.

Your Countermeasure:
When you second-guess yourself, look at your notebook for your original intentions and your thoughts on unity. Go back and review the section on "making decisions from either fear or intuition." Have courage, take appropriate risks and listen to your intuition.

CHAPTER 17
DARKEST SECRET #17: EXPECT BAD ADVICE.

Any time you talk about the look of the film, it's not just the director and the director of photography. You have to include the costume designer and the production designer. - Spike Lee, writer-director of Malcolm X *and* Do the Right Thing

While your department heads will make a significant contribution, it is still the director's responsibility to pull everything together to make an artistic whole.

Why would anyone give you bad advice? Because they can only see their small bit of the production. They don't see the whole context. That's your job as the director.

I had a conversation with some industry professionals and the following categories of "bad advice" arose:

1) Incompetence

If you listen carefully, you'll often notice that individuals will take one detail, toss in a lot of guesses, then fervently hold a position. For example, a friend severely criticized the

TV series *Dexter*. I asked, "Have you seen an episode?" She said, "No" and continued her complaining without a pause.

2) Their vision is in conflict with yours, the director.

Sometimes people are "not making the same movie." By that I mean, their personal objectives and preferences do not mesh. There needs to be one vision—yours—so the film will feel like a coherent, well-structured work. Sometimes, when certain people apply to work for me, I can sense that they have a rigid vision of their own. It would drain too much of my energy to attempt to justify my choices to their satisfaction. But that's not what I'm there to do. I'm there to create the best film I can. My intuition speaks loudly that these applicants are not on the same page with me. I do not hire them.

You're the director. Ultimately, your intuition must guide the project.

3. Political, religious, or "personal gain" agendas.

Watch out for hidden agendas. For example, studio executives (with a personal gain agenda) often want to get "their fingerprints" on a project. So they may offer detrimental revisions on a script. A number of studio executives also just want to protect their position. They want to just package a project (with stars, a noted screenwriter, a particular genre) so that they can say, "Well, it should have worked. I mean, I had all the elements in place."

How do you handle advice from a studio executive? You hear them out and take notes. Sometimes, you'll have a happy outcome when you ignore the bad advice, but the studio executive is distracted with how pleased he is with some other element of the film. And sometimes, situations lead to no happy ending. Look at Terry Gilliam's film *Brazil* that led to years of litigation as the producers tried to turn it into a more conventional movie. Or Ridley Scott's *Blade Runner* that was also re-edited by the studio with a voiceover "explaining" the story and a happy ending tacked on. As one of my editors of this book said, "There's a dark secret for you—sometimes you just don't win." That may be true. But both *Brazil* and *Blade Runner* have director's cuts on DVD and Blu-ray that reveal the director's original intentions.

4. Ordinary human error.

We all make mistakes. But some people are not open to learn from them. Dr. Henry Cloud writes about "wise people, foolish people and evil people." We'll focus on the bad advice coming from foolish people. Some years ago, I hired a videographer to film a speech that I gave. When I saw the final footage I was gravely disappointed. In a calm voice, during a phone conversation, I said, "So how can we do better next time?" Suddenly, this videographer was cursing and carrying on. I had carefully said "we" because I had sincerely wanted to learn from errors I made and that he had made. He pushed himself, in my eyes, to the "foolish people" category. So when you hear advice, consider the source. Is this someone who learns from errors? Are they making an error about the intent of the film you are directing? And be careful to spot whether you're talking to a "foolish person."

So how do you deal with any advice? First, hear the person out (unless you have a dire situation like racing the loss of sunlight at the end of the day). Why? There are moments when you'll find "bad" advice turns out to be good. When director Steven Frears did *Dangerous Liaisons*, actor John Malkovitch wanted to do a scene a certain way that Frears didn't like. So they did multiple takes, including letting Malkovitch do his thing. Looking at the dailies Malkovitch was right—it worked better for him to be a little physically brutal with Michelle Pfeiffer's character. The screenwriter for *The King's Speech* told a story about how the producers wanted to increase the screen time given to the Abdication Crisis. He calmly did as they liked, trusting in their competence to come around to what he already realized—that such an emphasis threw the whole film out of focus.

When you hear advice, consider these questions:
- Does this help me serve my target market?
- Is this just an expression of ego on the part of the comment maker?
- Is this personal? That is, does the comment-maker want to hurt me?
- Does the comment-maker want to get me to second guess myself?
- Does the comment-maker have real and useful knowledge in the area we're discussing?
- Does the comment-maker have a hidden agenda?

Sometimes, when you feel that no one agrees with you, it helps to look at both your original intentions (in your notes) and your thoughts about whether the advice is truly helpful. (You can return to the questions above.) A number of industry professionals I know find it helpful to write out their thoughts in a journal. It's easier to see what is true and what is noise, when it's on paper.

Points to Remember:

Darkest Secret #17: Expect bad advice.

Your Countermeasure:

In your own mind, submit advice to these questions:
- Does this help me serve my target market?
- Is this just an expression of ego on the part of the comment-maker?
- Is this personal? That is, does the comment-maker want to hurt me?
- Does the comment-maker wants to get me to second guess myself?
- Does the comment-maker have real and useful knowledge in the area we're discussing?
- Does the comment-maker have a hidden agenda?

CHAPTER 18
DARKEST SECRET #18: TAKE CARE OF YOURSELF (NO ONE ELSE WILL).

An interviewer asked Steven Spielberg what someone should do to prepare for directing. "Go to the gym," Spielberg said. He holds that a director needs to be physically strong to endure the rigors of his or her job.

Walter Murch, a celebrated film editor, began directing *Return to Oz* with high hopes. Murch reportedly had a nervous breakdown five weeks into the shoot. Let's remember that directors are under so much pressure because they more than anyone are held responsible for a film's success or failure. George Lucas came to Murch's aid and got the production back on track. Then, Steven Spielberg and Francis Ford Coppola joined in and helped Murch. It's good to have top level friends!

Now, it may seem that this story of friends coming to the aid of Murch is counter to the topic of this section: "Take care of yourself." My intent in sharing this story is to demonstrate that the stress of filmmaking can be overwhelming. Hence, you must take care of yourself.

Earlier, I mentioned having a support system and the value of exercise and a hobby that allows one to decompress (even just for fifteen minutes).

I have talked with filmmaking professionals about how they take care of themselves. Here are some of their methods:
- A walk during lunchtime
- A brief nap at lunchtime
- Lots of water through the day
- "I decompress by playing my violin in my trailer."
- "I meditate for ten minutes in the morning."
- "I rub my feet with sesame oil."
- "I call my brother at the end of the day. We share some laughs."

The film industry is a tough place with both artistic and other pressures. Although he's not a director, Robert Downey Jr., the actor, may be an example of an artist who nearly lost it all due to various pressures. Downey Jr. says that he has been drug-free since July 2003. He developed a whole support system that includes:
- time with family
- therapy (counseling)
- meditation
- twelve-step recovery program
- yoga
- the practice of Wing Chun Kung Fu

It's up to you to find the support you need. The film industry is a tough place. You must be tough, and having a support system is essential.

I discussed this chapter with friends in the film and

television industry and they raised some topics related to "take care of yourself." They said things like: "Will you also deal with the cutthroat nature of show business and how a director can protect himself?" Here are some of the topics:

How to protect yourself from being "pushed out"

It's reported that Catherine Hardwicke, the director of the first film in the *Twilight* franchise, was pushed out. The producers simply reduced her budget on the sequel until she knew making the film would be impossible. Then the budget soared once a new director was hired.

What can you do? Sometimes, not much. Although it is a cliché, sometimes "creative differences" are truly a factor. I always remember what Lynda Obst (producer of *Sleepless in Seattle*) told me, "Be someone they want along for the ride." She had been pushed out of the production of *Flashdance*, although she had originated the project.

Otherwise, the director can empower himself or herself by being cordial with the producers. Do your best to avoid yelling around the producers even when you're deeply frustrated. Also show some flexibility. In any negotiation, the other side wants to "see some movement." For example, director Gore Verbinski, producer Jerry Bruckheimer and stars Johnny Depp and Armie Hammer agreed to take a pay cut of 20% to entice Disney to go forward with the film *The Lone Ranger*. The budget went from $250 million down to $215 million. There was some movement.

Further, do your best to stay on schedule and avoid going over budget.

How to protect yourself from the studio interfering and twisting your film

Some industry insiders say that director Joel Schumacher

allowed himself to be talked into making *Batman and Robin* as "toy friendly" as possible. The result? A movie that killed the franchise and damaged Schumacher's reputation.

What can you do? Get strategic about negotiating. (To learn more about negotiating, please consider another book in this series entitled *Darkest Secrets of Negotiating Masters: How to Protect Yourself* . . .). Preplan what concessions you'll make and what you won't give up. We'll never know what truly happened in the meetings for *Batman and Robin*. I'll suggest that it may have helped if Schumacher could have negotiated the concessions in this way: "Okay. I'll keep the 'silly hockey fight scene,' but I want to limit Arnold Schwarzenegger's 'Mr. Freeze puns' to only two."

It's entirely possible that Schumacher found himself in an impossible place with too much pressure from all sides. Did Schwarzenegger insist on all the "Mr. Freeze puns" dialogue? Viewers of the film told me they found it grating to hear Schwarzenegger (as Mr. Freeze) saying: "You're not sending me to the cooler!" and "Ice to see you!" and . . . no! That's enough. [Okay, one more: "Tonight, hell freezes over."]

Many times, if you turn in a film on time and under budget, you can get away with a lot.

This appears to be writer-director Robert Rodriguez's strategy. He basically makes his multi-million dollar films at home (in his home studio with editing, music soundtrack recording and other equipment). He consistently makes money for the studios. And they appear to leave him alone to do his work. His first film El Mariachi cost $7,000 and later the studio probably added around $50,000 for more sound mixing. *El Mariachi* earned over $2 million at the domestic box office. His next film *Desperado* (budget $7 million) made $25.4 million at the domestic box office. And so on.

Develop your opportunities for leverage.

Peter Jackson launched a lawsuit against New Line Cinema because he felt the company failed to pay him a fair portion from merchandising, video and computer games releases associated with the first film *The Fellowship of the Ring*. Eventually things worked out for Jackson. Why? New Line Cinema ultimately wanted Jackson to produce and direct the next two films *The Hobbit: An Unexpected Journey* and *The Hobbit: There and Back Again*. (It's true that for a time Guillermo del Toro was hired as the director, but it was not until Jackson signed as director that the project was officially greenlit.)

Where does leverage start? With whoever owns the rights to the material. Jackson never gave up the rights to his screenplay of *The Lord of the Rings*, so when Miramax wanted to make it one film instead of two they found themselves holding rather fewer cards than they thought.

Hire the best lawyer you can. And hold on to as many rights to a project as you can.

In 2000, writer-director Terry Gilliam lost the rights to his screenplay *The Man Who Killed Don Quixote* when production of the film was cancelled due to on-set mishaps. For the next six years, Gilliam struggled to regain rights to his screenplay, dealing with legalities between the French producers and German insurers. Finally, Gilliam began main pre-production in 2009. Then *Variety* reported on September 5, 2010 that Terry Gilliam revealed that funding had collapsed about two months before filming started.

So to protect yourself: take care of your own health, learn about negotiation strategies, hire the best lawyer you can, protect your rights to material and develop some leverage. What will happen? Sometimes you'll win and sometimes you'll lose. Make sure you find ways to learn every time and you'll get stronger and closer to making your dreams come true.

Points to Remember:

Darkest Secret #18: Take care of yourself (no one else will).

Your Countermeasure:
Identify ten things you can do to support yourself. Will you program regular exercise, good nutrition, counseling, meditation, a hobby or some other ways to decompress? And, focus on strengthening your position in the business by learning about negotiation strategies, hiring the best lawyer you can, protecting your rights to material and developing some leverage.

CHAPTER 19
DARKEST SECRET #19: REMEMBER — A PRODUCER CAN FIRE YOU AT ANY TIME.

As I mentioned earlier in this book, producer Lynda Obst was fired from the film *Flashdance* even though she had originated the project. She told me, "Be someone they want along for the ride." She was referring to other producers and studio executives. Lynda Obst went on to produce hits like *Sleepless* in *Seattle and Contact*.

As a side note, I asked Obst what brings her fulfillment and she replied, "Writing."

Imagine that you can empower yourself to reduce the chance of being fired. How? My father has a phrase he likes to say: "Don't let them get a handle on you." What would be that handle? Two things in particular: a) if you don't get your shots (get behind schedule) and b) if you go over budget.

Here are seven methods to ensure that you get your shots:

1) Change to quicker camera setups.

One way to get more shots in less time is to use a steadicam. Another way, if you have actors who mesh well, is to use a wider shot to get more of the cast in.

2) Avoid laying tracks for complicated dolly shots.

Years ago, when stuck with a modest budget, I used a "cameraperson in a wheelchair method." This works for getting quick shots of someone running.

3) Use two cameras simultaneously.

I prefer to have one camera on a close-up of one actor and then have the other camera doing an over-the-shoulder shot favoring the other actor.

4) Edit the movie in your head and avoid retaking shots.

For one film, I watched as a jet ski stuntman wiped out with a big splash. But I did *not* call for another take of the stunt because I knew that I could cut away and assemble the shots. It worked so well that some industry professionals demanded to know: "How did you do that jet ski stunt?"

Spielberg saved time by having detailed storyboards done before being on the set of *Raiders of the Lost Ark*. He brought in the film about 15 days early! You can save a lot of time by using software to "pre-viz" (pre-visualize) your shots. The good thing about having such animated images is that your department heads (and actors) can literally see what you're aiming to achieve.

5) Avoid filming on water, or with children or animals.

Yes, this piece of advice is a cliché. Yes, we can all give examples where wildly successful and beloved films broke this rule—from *Jaws* to *Titanic* to *Aliens* and *The Wizard of Oz*, and so on. Avoid doing it anyway. At first. All three elements take too much time because they're unpredictable. Try to have a second unit film close-ups of animals. For example, there is an amazing shot in the film *The Diary of Anne Frank*, directed by George Stevens. A cat gets his head stuck in a metal funnel and at any moment that funnel can drop from its head and crash to the floor. Such a clamor would alert the German soldiers to capture and kill the Jewish people hiding in the room. Such a suspenseful moment. How did they get the shot? Director David Mamet has a theory: before principal photography, the second unit can use five cameras filming five different cats with duplicates of the cats. Whatever cat that did something amazing would be placed in the movie (with his double). Mamet called up Stevens's son to confirm how the shot was done. George Stevens, Jr. confirmed that there were a bunch of cats and an extreme amount of footage as the cameraman waited for any cat to do something "uncatlike." I share this story to confirm just how much trouble it is to get one shot when working with animals.

6) Use what you have to do "double work."

It had been a long day and my co-star had left to get some needed rest. I was still shooting—both directing and acting. I suddenly felt a surge of intense emotion in Scene 60. I filmed the scene and realized that I could use that emotion to shoot a close-up of me for Scene 81. Only a close-up because my co-star was at home and asleep. [This is what I mean about doing "double work."]

So with tears falling from my eyes, I said, "Get me a white wall." My co-producer looked at me like I had lost my mind. "A white wall?" I told them it was for Scene 81 now and we were going to film my close-up. The crew placed a white wall behind me in minutes and we shot the intense scene in which my character, a Vietnamese boatperson shared a heart-wrenching story of a mother on the boat and her surviving child crying inconsolably. So I used my own emotions to do two powerful scenes. I call that "use what you have to do double work."

Let's continue with this "double work" idea. If you design your film so that it takes place over two days, you can keep your actors in one set of clothes. Then you can film scenes from different parts of the script in the same location—while avoiding lost time to wardrobe changes. This works especially well if the clothes do not get torn during the course of the story.

7) Minimize travel time (find serviceable locations).

Some directors insist on the perfect locations and perfect weather. I don't. I'll set things up so that I just turn the camera 180 degrees (facing the other direction) and now I'll have a different street to film on. My intention is to minimize travel time. Less travel means more camera setups per day. About stopping for weather: If it starts to rain during a scene, you can cut away to raindrops starting to fall on a puddle to create a transition to rough weather. Similarly, I had a scene in which a printer blows up. We were filming quickly and did not manage to get a transitional shot between when the characters were in clean clothes and then were covered in ink after the explosion. The budget was tight. No time or money for a reshoot. What to do? I had a second unit shoot a close-up of ink hitting a wall. So when I went to the two-shot of the characters, it was clear why they were covered in ink.

8) Get your whole team thinking "do more with less."

Study behind the scenes material found on DVDs, Blu-rays and books for examples of productions that got things done quickly and for low cost. The makers of the film The Specials shot almost the entire film in one house in Los Feliz. The film *Monty Python and the Holy Grail* seems to include visits to no less than five castles. In fact, four of those five were the same place, shot from different angles. The old *Flash Gordon* serials used the lab equipment from *Frankenstein* and stuck one character in the Cowardly Lion's costume from *Wizard of Oz*. One film created a gunfight without showing any guns! The would-be victims hid in a dark room. Bullet holes began to appear in the wall, creating beams of light. Similarly, early film noir movies created some spectacular effects with stylized blocking simply because they lacked funds for extra film. Tell these kinds of stories to your department heads and ask people to give you five ideas each.

Finally, there is a useful solution to the getting fired problem. Insist on being one of the producers (when you have the clout to do so). As a producer, you have leverage; you're no longer merely a "hired gun." Elia Kazan said about the first film he both produced and directed, "There was less tension."

Points to Remember:

Darkest Secret #19: Remember—a producer can fire you at any time.

Your Countermeasure:
Use eight methods to get your shots:
1) Change to quicker camera setups.
2) Avoid laying tracks for complicated dolly shots.
3) Use two cameras simultaneously.

4) Edit the movie in your head and avoid retaking shots.
5) Avoid filming on water, or with children, or animals.
6) Use what you have to do "double work."
7) Minimize travel time (find serviceable locations).
8) Get your whole team thinking "do more with less."

CHAPTER 20
DARKEST SECRET #20: REMEMBER—A NAME ACTOR CAN GET A PRODUCER TO FIRE YOU AT ANY TIME.

Screenwriter Robert Towne initially got the job of directing *Two Jakes*, the sequel to the hugely successful Chinatown (which Towne had also written). Robert Evans, one of the film's producers, was lined up to be one of the two Jakes of the title. But he wasn't. It's said that Towne fired him. And then Towne himself got the boot. Actor Jack Nicholson stepped in as the new director.

What happened? Did Evans take offense and arrange for Towne's dismissal? Or did Jack Nicholson push to direct the film? Either scenario is plausible. That's how the film industry works.

For the film *Robin Hood: Prince of Thieves*, star Kevin Costner fully supported the decision for his friend Kevin Reynolds as the director of the film. But during postproduction, the producers—including Costner—locked Reynolds out of the editing room.

All things considered, it counts as amazing that Costner invited Reynolds to direct *Waterworld* . . . and Reynolds accepted! But they fought again (like on *Robin Hood*) and Costner finished the film himself. Later, Reynolds said, "Kevin Costner should only act in movies he directs. That way, he can work with his favorite actor and director."

It's a scary fact that you as director, although considered supremely responsible for a movie's fate, do not in fact have the final word. As you can imagine, this fact is hard to take emotionally. I remember what producer Lynda Obst said to me, "Have a bunch of projects on the roof." She explained her metaphor as: with the vagaries of the film industry, that she pursues multiple projects. When something goes wrong, she either tosses a project "back up on the roof" or she "pulls another project down off the roof." My point is that when you have multiple projects going, you don't feel as desperate when one project is yanked out of your hands.

When working with a name actor, it's important to find out why the actor approved of you for the director in the first place. That's usually how it goes: In Hollywood, films are usually packaged. A package often comprises a screenplay plus a name actor and a director. At some point, you might ask the actor, "So what about my work had you thinking that I'd be a good match for this project?" You need to do this with finesse. It's better to start the conversation as a general discussion of favorite films and esteemed performances.

The name actor (or "star") probably has a favorite among the films. Find out why that film is a favorite. You can ask, "What about [your film's name] worked for you?" (People in the industry often talk about "Is it working?")

Then on set you can use this knowledge when you're guiding the name actor to a performance. You might say, "Remember the part of *Red Engine,* when the hero expressed, just for a moment, his heartfelt reason to take on Drenden? That's similar to this situation. So here's how I can help you get to a moment like that. . ."

The point is that any name actor is two things: highly ambitious and likely scared.

Why scared? In an interview, Sylvester Stallone said it was better when he was climbing to the top. "You never knew when you might get a break. But it's harder just to stay at the top." Some people assume that actors who seem arrogant have no fear. But many prove to be afraid and arrogance became a defense mechanism. A mask to hide behind.

It is scary for an actor when you get hired as a lead. No matter what the plot is, it is your job to do something interesting enough to make them want to get inside the lead character's head.
- Tom Selleck, actor

So you as the director, in the name actor's eyes, are a tool to help him or her stay at the top or perhaps, do even better. You want to avoid being perceived as an obstacle. What do people do with obstacles? Avoid them. Unless you cannot. Then what? Then, obstacles are removed.

Think about the industry. An actor starts at the bottom and is kicked around.

Then some lucky break happens—the actor is cast in a career-making role. Some examples: Judy Garland in *Wizard of Oz*. Al Pacino in *The Godfather*. Marisa Tomei in *My Cousin Vinny*.

Suddenly, everything changes. A nobody now has power—and probably no real idea how to use it. People who ignored this person now fawn over them. Paparazzi follow their every move. Questions they'd never even considered end up thrown at them in interview after interview. Most feel at least a little unbalanced by the whole experience. Plenty feel extremely unbalanced. Think of Marilyn Monroe, James Dean, Marlon Brando, Veronica Lake and Lindsay Lohan.

I was trained to be an actor, not a star. I was trained to play roles, not to deal with fame and agents and lawyers and the press.
- Gene Hackman, actor

It's definitely nerve-racking to be the center of attention. I'm not the kind of an actor that just craves attention 24-7 - but it's part of the deal. - Jon Hamm, actor

Who can the name actor trust? You. Part of your job is to be someone the star can trust. What does that mean? More importantly, how do you achieve such a thing? You can start by being respectful, as well as worthy of respect.

Much of this book talks about asking gentle questions and listening. That's part of being respectful. Further, you need to treat each actor as an individual. Each actor has his or her own process. Some love to rehearse. Others hate it. Some are so into the Method they seem to drown in the part. Still others drop the character completely when the director says, "Cut!" There are actors who need to be handled with kid gloves while others long to be challenged. Some find it the worst kind of unprofessionalism to keep the actors and crew late, while others cannot stand it if the director is not a grinding perfectionist. And you need to treat each one differently.

The worthy of respect part includes:
- You have a clear vision.
- You've done your homework.
- You come across as a real professional (on time, consistent in doing what you'll say you do).
- You treat others with respect.

But let's face it. Any name actor almost certainly has an

entourage and if you happen to get on the bad side of one of those, that person is likely to badmouth you.

How do you solve something like that? Do your best to talk directly to the actor. And avoid leaving important details as messages that any of the entourage will be "passing on" to the actor.

Fortunately I learned this lesson without making a movie. The hard way, but I learned it. I was working as a contractor for a major corporation. The company was being swallowed in a merger, and my duties had been rendered moot. So I told my boss' executive assistant that I would "stay on call"—so if there was work for me to do, to just call me. Big mistake! Can you spot it? I did not at the time. But then, what is youth for? That assistant did not pass along my message. More, when questioned about it, he lied. With hindsight, I now realize the thing to do was go directly to the vice president, asking his specific approval for the idea of being "on call."

Translate that situation onto a film set. Imagine all kinds of ways the same mistake might play out while communicating with a performer and his entourage. Now plan against ever making the same mistake.

Here's another important subject when dealing with a name actor: "Dailies" (unedited footage). Do you allow actors to view the dailies? When name actors wants to view dailies, they get their way. Why? Any name actor often has the most power in the room. Certainly more power than the director and producer—unless one is named Steven Spielberg or Jerry Bruckheimer.

You can say, "Sure. See you at 6 pm." Often an actor will attend a couple of dailies viewing sessions and then stop, not attending any more. Or return only now and then. Watching dailies makes for a dull few hours of time. (Years later Peter Jackson still groaned about watching hour after hour of footage of horses riding around for Fellowship of the Ring.) Here's a good tip: Be sure to talk with your editing team and frontload good takes for the beginning of the session. Since we're all doing things digitally—it won't take too long for the editing team to get you the best footage. Why? Hopefully, the actor will see the good takes and—wait for it—leave!

Name actors tend to want to take a look at the monitor on set. Okay. Certain name actors like to see the director looking directly at the acting and not at the monitor. It will make you stand out. Why? Because many directors now are "technical directors"—so they're staring at the monitor all the time. The "actor's director" sits near the camera and watches the performance.

As a side note, I prefer to look directly at the acting. I want to concentrate on the acting and not the framing of the scene. (I tend to draw quick storyboards to show the director of photography/camera operator what I want to see in terms of framing. I also check playback of footage to see if what I meant by close-up is what the camera operator accomplished.)

A number of name actors have praised their directors with: "Yes. He sits right next to the camera. Not behind the monitor."

Finally, I'll share with you some details about influencing people. The director does not control an actor. The director influences the actor. Some directors make the mistake of coming up with an idea and then "trying to sell" an actor on that idea. It's better to start from a whole different point of view. Influence is about helping the actors experience the situation and come upon insights themselves. To illustrate some foundational ideas about influence, I'll now share questions that Dr. Michael V. Pantalon writes in his book, Instant Influence, about as part of the process of influence—that he has verified with various studies. He writes that the process of influencing people is divided into six steps:

Step 1: Why might you [the actor] change?

Step 2: How ready are you to change—on a scale of 1 to 10, where 1 means 'not ready at all' and 10 mean 'totally ready'?

Step 3: Why didn't you pick a lower number?

Step 4: Imagine you've changed. What would the positive outcomes be?

Step 5: Why are those outcomes important to you?

Step 6: What's the next step, if any?

Why would these six steps be relevant to you as a director? A director must be a master of influence. Now I invite you to go to a deeper level of influence. You know your own answers and the direction you want for a scene. But if you just say them as pronouncements, the actor can brush them off. You need to guide the actor to his or her own values and to personal insights needed to improve the performance.

Now, trained actors and directors may find the above "Six Steps" questions to be stilted, and Dr. Pantalon has handled such an objection by providing numerous variations in his book *Instant Influence*. From studying Pantalon's book, I was inspired to describe some principles of influencing people in this way:

1) People do what they do for their reasons—not yours.

2) To be a master of influence, you need to ask questions to get the person to experience and recognize her own values and her own reasons to do something.

3) Lecturing people is ineffective.

4) People learn what they want, often, by expressing the desire out loud.

We realize that the director knows where she'd like the scene to go. But she avoids making pronouncements because the actor may resist going there. No one likes being dragged by the nose. We're talking about the art of influence. You would not use the exact above "Six Steps" questions. Instead, an interaction with a name actor might go this way:

The Scene: Sam's upset. The woman he thought was his girlfriend has been using him. And she just told him flat out.

> Director: So Sam, how do you see the character here?
> Sam (name actor): He's pissed!
> Director: What's another word for that?
> Sam: He's angry.
> Director: What's another word?
> Sam: Enraged. I feel like a volcano going off.
> Director: If a volcano could talk, how would it?
> Sam: It erupts. Roaring. Spewing flame.
> Director: Is it erupting or getting ready to erupt?
> Sam: Erupting, of course.
> Director: Okay, let's do a take.
> [They film a take.]
> Director: How did that feel?
> Sam: Good. Like I got everything off my chest.
> Director: Okay, so that's the end of the movie. The story is over.
> Sam: Well, no.
> Director: So what happens before an eruption?
> Sam: It rumbles. There's an earthquake.

You can see how the director makes sure that the actor has an experience. Maybe the above direction or image would not be appropriate for another scene or for different actors. You can find something else that will. You might help the actor look for a sense memory. Something in the past. And maybe invite the actor to "make it worse."

Successful directors often help an actor find something that comes from the name actor's own values, goals and feelings.

In summary, identify what the name actor likes about your previous work. Take care about dailies. Learn to influence by asking questions that help the name actor have experiences and insights.

Points to Remember:

Darkest Secret #20: Remember—a name actor can get a producer to fire you at any time.

Your Countermeasure:
When you work with a name actor, you need to be both respectful and worthy of respect. You do your homework so you have a clear vision of what you want to see in a scene. But then you influence the actor by asking questions and helping the actor have experiences and insights. You look upon the actor as a true collaborator, and you take the film to a higher level as you truly work together.

CHAPTER 21
DARKEST SECRET #21: PLAN TO COMPENSATE FOR YOUR TENDENCIES.

As a director you have to be careful you don't over-design the film. You have to be careful that the period aspect does not take over. - Stanley Tucci, actor and director

Every filmmaker has some automatic tendencies. Often we see that excellent films come out of the give-and-take between collaborators.

Then, at times, trouble can happen when a director gives in to some disruptive personal tendencies. Hollywood still rocks with tales of director Michael Cimino's excesses when making *Heaven's Gate*.

An example of effective collaboration is when one of the producers of *The Sixth Sense* pushed director M. Night Shyamalan to including a sequence of shots that explain that ... **Spoiler Alert** ... the Bruce Willis character was actually dead throughout the whole film. What was the collaboration? The producer brought new ideas and a different point of view to Shyamalan's attention. The Sixth Sense would have truly a different form without a producer to provide some input.

I've talked with a number of industry people who say that M. Night Shyamalan's work has suffered in recent years because he has had more clout and has not had strong producers to push him to revise certain elements of his recent films. It appears that no one keeps Shyamalan's tendencies in check. Several industry people feel the same about George Lucas, who apparently had no one in his circle to really object to what many consider big mistakes with Jar Jar Binks and the sneaky villains with Asian voices (at the beginning of *Star Wars: Episode One - The Phantom Menace*).

Some years ago, I directed one of my first films and did the first cut according to my own sensibilities. Tight cuts with short, quick shots. Fortunately, I showed the cut to another director, and he told me something I needed to hear, that a good film has multiple rhythms. Even fast cutting becomes monotonous. What was the solution? For my next project I had two people with me in the editing room for the final edit. I wanted that give and take.

I tend to emphasize a phrase: "Know your tendencies and compensate for them."

The effective director uses whatever tools will help. The filmmaking process often flows forward in a surprising direction. If the film seems to require a new approach, then the director may need to be truly flexible.

A director shouldn't get in the way of the movie, the story should. - Frank Darabont, director of
   The Shawshank Redemption *and* The Green Mile

Remember your number one job: tell the story well. And

sometimes, a scene will be so powerful on the set that it sends ripple effects throughout the rest of the film. On one film, I discovered that a father-daughter scene gained new power on the set. During the scene, I staged a moment in which the father "John" watched his daughter taken away by his brother. The moment had a moving resonance. John was upside down in his life, drinking and sleeping on park benches while his brother was caring for his half-Vietnamese daughter. As the brother took his daughter to another room to get her lunch, it was as if time slowed down. The daughter waved at her daddy then looked downward. The look on John's face expressed his self-reproach and anguish.

I saw it on the set. I had to rewrite the ending of the story. This dynamic was just too powerful. So that night, I rewrote the ending and we filmed new scenes the next day.

My point is that as a director, I compensated for something that I had missed as the screenwriter.

You need trusted advisors who can help you compensate for your natural tendencies. For example, on *Field of Dreams*, writer-director Phil Alden Robinson had an advocate in his star Kevin Costner. Costner said, "[Phil,]You're going to hear that this script should be changed. I'm going to be there saying don't change the script."

How do you get trustworthy help? First off, don't snarl every time someone disagrees with you or offers criticism. Why? It hurts to get angry resistance if one is "just trying to help." So many people just avoid the pain and keep their mouths shut. It's true that plenty of the time you need to stick to your guns no matter what, but at least as often someone is giving a genuine piece of wisdom. You'll have to decide which, but doing that requires listening.

Invite your most trusted team members to take you aside and talk about vital details. You want conversation. I'm

NOT saying "let them walk all over you." You need to maintain the chain of command. And, elsewhere in this book, I talk about the time I had to take a producer aside and insist that the actors hear one voice, the director's voice. (That producer had been directing on set. I had to nip that in the bud.)

Learn to use the powerful tool of "and."

For example, a director Mark said, "Sarah, that's an interesting point. I'll talk with you about it in a couple of moments. And, we're going to keep up the pace. We'll get another take right now."

Notice that Mark said "And" and not "but." The word "but" causes trouble because it makes everything before it sound like a "lie." The most vivid way I can explain this is with an example: "Jimmy, you're a good kid, but your room is messy." What does Jimmy think? "My room is messy so I must not be a good kid."

Develop a number of phrases that encourage input.

Before sharing two phrases, I feel it necessary to emphasize that you need to look the actor in the eye and communicate your sincerity. I have had actors view sections of this book and some were quick to jump on a rough-draft sentence and call it a "brush off." How do you avoid that problem? Sincerity and body language. So you're going to need to stop, look the actor in the eye and let your sincerity enrich the tone of your voice. You could express appreciation for input with something like: "I'm glad you brought that up." Sometimes, I'll say, "I'm going to need to think about that. Serena, I can see how important that is to you. I'll get back to you. How about we revisit this at 5 PM?" And I write down in my schedule to have that conversation—and I write a few notes. And I have the actor see me make my notes. Let's face it. Some actors are high strung, and they need to be reassured that you're taking them and their concerns seriously.

Elsewhere in this book, I mentioned Spielberg's comment: "A good director knows when to say 'yes.'" My thought is: "A good director creates an atmosphere where there's a lot to say 'yes' to." And this is how I compensate for my own tendencies, by getting input and feedback from team members. Then I can make informed decisions.

I often ask for comments before I mention my own views. I don't want people to self-censor—which they often do in the face of a director making some "pronouncements."

At the same time, convey that you know where you want the film to go. For example, on the set, I invited the actors to suggest a quick line to act as a "button" to a comedic moment. A couple suggested some lines. I replied, "We're getting close. I'm looking for a certain rhythm. It needs to be shorter." With those last two sentences, I conveyed my own clarity. Team members want to hear the confidence a director has.

So the idea is that the director knows where we're going. And he or she may ask for input on how to get there. And that's how the director compensates for his or her tendencies.

Directors face a deluge of input from so many people that, as human beings, they miss subtleties. With that in mind, I talked with some actors about directors' tendencies that frustrate them.

1) Defusing things with humor, even when the tone on set makes that inappropriate

Let's face it. If you're feeling upset, someone trying to "jolly you out of it" will likely make you furious. Making films is a serious undertaking. People's careers are riding on their performance. There's plenty of fear. So let your actors and crew know that you take their concerns seriously.

2) Playing favorites with the cast and crew

This one is a trap that's easy to fall into. Why? Some people rub us the "right way." And we naturally tend to be nice to those individuals. It helps to be known as "firm and fair." Crews can get nervous if it seems that the director lets himself be walked on by everyone. So you need to take a firm tone, at times. And watch your own behavior. Are you granting special favors just to the people you like? Stop that. Be fair.

3) Taking comments personally

Artists, whether they're actors or crew, can be passionate, loud and unreasonable. You need a thick skin. You're the director; you can't let yourself stay moody if someone insults you. It's all about getting things done through people's efforts. At the same time, you need to maintain a chain of command. You can take an angry cinematographer aside and say, "I can see you're frustrated with me. You can tell me all about it. And I require that we do not disrupt the crew. We're talking about this over here. I'm listening to you."

4) Ignoring the emotional pulse of other people

If someone is upset, it's not "just going to go away." When I talk about asking questions and listening, I do NOT mean avoiding conflict. I mean being skilled at confronting situations. You go in and face the situation, but you do not escalate it. As I said earlier, you can say something like, "I can see you're frustrated with me..."

5) Going off on tangents

This can be a tough situation for some directors. Certainly, you're excited to be directing your film and you love to talk about filmmaking. But realize that a lot of people are preoccupied with their personal problems and they are not hanging on your every word. I learned this powerfully in another arena. I teach graduate students, and every year, I attend a workshop or two as a student myself. Why? I learn something new. But I also see how boring it can be to hear someone else (the professor) talking and talking and . . .

So pay attention. Listen to yourself and especially watch the faces of people you're addressing. Are their eyes glazing over? Watch their body language. Are they fidgeting? Restrain yourself. Say what you need to say concisely.

Points to Remember:

Darkest Secret #21: Plan to compensate for your tendencies.

Your Countermeasure:

Encourage input. And still convey your confidence that you know where the film needs to go. You inviting trusted team members to help you with the how it gets there. Also, beware of directors' tendencies that frustrate actors and crew:

1) Defusing things with humor, even when the tone on set makes that inappropriate

2) Playing favorites with the cast and crew

3) Taking comments personally
4) Ignoring the emotional pulse of other people
5) Going off on tangents.

SECTION TWO:
USE THE D.I.R.E.C.T. SYSTEM

This section is a compilation of responses I have made both in interviews and in response to questions posted by my graduate students.

Tom, can you summarize some of the most important things a new director should have in mind?

I emphasize the D.I.R.E.C.T. System:

D – do preparation
I – inquire with experts
R – respond in the moment
E – express confidence
C – cover the possibilities
T – target necessary footage

1. Do preparation
For one of my feature films, I personally drew 805

storyboards. Some of my favorite moments in the film are based on those storyboards. For example, one scene starts with one character, "Son," asleep and the camera tilts down to darkness. The scene shifts to the night sky and the camera tilts down and finally rests on "John" the main character, fitfully sleeping on a park bench. This seamless transition began with my sketching the storyboards. You can bet that I knew the movie in depth.

Director M. Night Shyamalan did storyboards (with an artist) three times for *Signs* (starring Mel Gibson) before he shot one frame of the film.

Before he films his movies, Francis Ford Coppola conducts a staged reading in which actors perform the script like a play while they hold the script in hand.

I also do staged readings and shoot video of the actors. Sometimes, I gather an audience to view the staged reading and then I shoot video of the discussion session with the audience to capture the ideas and lessons learned. For one of my films, I discovered that the audience wanted a doctor's office scene, even though I was thoroughly against having such a scene. My solution was to film the scene in a manner that broke the usual mold of having the patient holding hands with a loved one while a doctor makes pronouncements. Instead, I had my main character alone facing a gruff doctor and I kept the doctor's face hidden until the end of the scene.

2. Inquire with experts

When I say "inquire with experts," I mean ask questions (inquire) and explore options by talking with people with specialized knowledge. One of the best things I did for one of my feature films was to show a rough cut to an effective editor who had nothing to do with the production. Her perspective was fresh, and she noticed that a character came across as shallow. This inspired me to go back and film pickups (extra shots that you go back and film. In essence, you pick up these shots).

It is also helpful to study books and DVDs about the making of feature films. For example, I learned that Gale Anne Hurd (producer of *Terminator*, *The Abyss*, *Aliens* and *Tremors*) co-authored the screenplay for the first feature film in the *Terminator* franchise. To accomplish her objectives on a movie set, Gale Anne Hurd said, "I always have a Plan B and C." She said, "I'm just attracted to the action element of science fiction. It's great to sit in the editing room with the director and sound engineers and create the feeling where your heart is racing and you're sitting at the edge of your seat and you find yourself holding your breath."

You can learn from listening to a director's commentary track on a DVD or Blu-ray. On the commentary track of The Godfather, director Francis Ford Coppola shares how he protected his position as director. As a young director, he noticed a number of indications that he might be replaced with a veteran director. In fact, Producer Robert Evans said that Coppola had no experience in directing action. The producer wanted to bring in a veteran action director. To combat this, on the weekend, Coppola had his young son and sister, Talia Shire, improvise the violent marital argument scene of *The Godfather*. He choreographed with them the camera moves and crashing dishes. Monday morning Coppola was prepared to film the scene on the set. Evans dropped the idea of bringing in the veteran action scene director. So preparation saved Coppola's job.

3. Respond in the moment

Producer Dino De Laurentiis said, "[Director] Ridley Scott

reminds me of Fellini . . . Some directors just film the script. [Like Fellini] Ridley adds to it on the set." Orson Welles talked about presiding over "happy accidents."

For one of my feature films, I directed an early scene in which a father, "John," was separated from his daughter temporarily. The power of the scene inspired me to rewrite the ending of the film, which we then filmed the next day. As I mentioned earlier in this book, I knew that such intensity at the beginning of the film required that John grow strong and have a resolution with his daughter. This all began with my responding to the power of one scene that played more intensely than I imagined when I first wrote the screenplay.

4. Express confidence

Actress Meryl Streep said, "Certainty is very attractive in people." Cast and crew need to trust that you know what you're doing. You need to give the impression that your vision is clear. You can get help from your actors, but still you need to express the main purpose of a scene. You can say something like: "In this scene, the brother needs to convey his hidden devotion to his kid brother." So you have clearly stated what you want to see. Then, you ask for input with something like: "The dialogue is not quite there yet. So Sam, how would the words come out of your character's mouth?"

One film director (whom an author kept as a confidential source) was known for the quick pace of his filming. He was considered quite confident. When he retired, he mentioned the secret for always looking confident and on top of things: he would have the actors do one extra take while he was thinking of the next thing to do. He would look in the direction of the actors, but his mind was handling the next step. Then at the end of the take, this director would say, "Good. Our next shot will be . . ."

5. Cover the possibilities

Successful directors "get coverage." Standard coverage for a dialogue scene between two characters is:
a) Close up of "Sam"
b) Close up of "Jennifer"
c) Over-the-shoulder shot favoring "Sam"
d) Over-the-shoulder shot favoring "Jennifer"
e) Two-shot
e) Master shot

The over-the-shoulder shot is designed to provide you with options in the editing room. Since we cannot see the mouth of the actor with his back to the camera, you can add lines of dialogue during postproduction.

A master shot is one that shows the whole bodies of the actors and the whole set (or location). Peter Weir, director of *Dead Poets Society*, only shoots part of a master shot—because he knows that he will continue the scene from closer-in.

Often, I will film a two-shot first because I do not want to waste the actors' best take on a master shot. A master shot usually misses a closer look at the actors' faces. Steven Spielberg often films the rehearsal in an effort to capture lightning in a bottle.

6. Target necessary footage

When I was filming at the San Luis Obispo Airport some years ago, I was assured by the airport officials that I had three hours to get the footage. But my intuition told me to do the crucial shots first. Sure enough, after one hour, I was asked to pack up the whole cast and crew and to leave. Fortunately, I had already filmed the "necessary footage." I had drawn storyboards, and I knew the vital shots.

By the way, I told the extras to leave the set, and I told the crew to fold up the lights and move them to the vehicles. Meanwhile I kept filming with the camera operator and the actors. At any point, if the airport officials inquired, I could reply: "See, we're leaving." I used one more technique. Since I was the co-star of the film, I left the final shots as close-ups of me. So during the last moments at the airport, I functioned as both director and actor with one camera operator. And then we left.

In *Section Three Make the Screenplay Excellent*, we will explore what a director needs to know about inspiring emotion in the audience.

SECTION THREE: MAKE THE SCREENPLAY EXCELLENT

1. What the Director Needs to Know about Inspiring Emotion In the Audience:

How can a director reliably inspire emotion in the audience?

First you connect with common experiences and common desires. Many people long for the loving support of a parent. For example, in *Million Dollar Baby* (starring and directed by Clint Eastwood), the Clint Eastwood character puts his soul at risk by deciding to help his surrogate daughter (portrayed by Hilary Swank in her Oscar®-winning role) in a particular way (I'll leave it to the film and avoid the spoiler here). Such incredible fatherly love is rare and precious.

So the audience is moved by longing for parental love.

We see the same thing in *Field of Dreams*. The main character gets a supernatural opportunity to have resolution and closure with his father.

What is another method to stir the audience's emotion?

Another powerful way to inspire the audience's emotion is a *Uniting for a Cause Scene*. An older film, *Batteries Not Included* (produced by Steven Spielberg) has an energizing scene that follows a sad scene. First, we get the sad scene in which one small flying robot tries to help a disabled man rebuild a hotel. The small flying robot comes across as a baby. Trying to help, the small 'baby' robot does what he can, but he is only able to place one tile at a time using his mouth. It appears that all is lost and that the hotel will be torn down. A few minutes later, the main characters look upward and hundreds of flying robots appear in the night sky, all arriving to help. What an exhilarating moment when viewing this film in the movie theater! I spoke with friends and they too felt joy at that moment. And I admit I had a few tears in my eyes on seeing that scene.

Here's another example of a rousing scene. In *Spartacus* (directed by Stanley Kubrick), Spartacus and his small group have been recaptured by Roman soldiers. Soldiers ask the recaptured slaves to identify Spartacus in exchange for leniency. Instead, in response to the soldier's question, one after another the slaves rise to their feet and say "I'm Spartacus" in an attempt to lay down their lives to protect Spartacus. This is a powerful showing of unity and esteem.

How about painful feelings?

In *Shrek*, the ogre, Shrek, stands outside a building and happens to overhear the Princess talking with Donkey about ugliness. Shrek assumes that the Princess is talking about his appearance. Feeling ugly in his own heart, Shrek throws away flowers he intended for the Princess. Actually, the Princess was talking about herself; and she really wanted a romantic relationship with Shrek. I call this the *Overhearing Words and Painful Misinterpretation Scene.*

How do you give the audience feelings of satisfaction?

You can focus on a Character Arc, which is the path of growth of the character during the story. Often when a director works with a screenwriter or when the director reviews the script on her own, she asks questions:
- How does the character grow?
- How does the character change during the course of the film?
- What does the character learn?

The character arc helps the audience with the character. And identifying with the main character, the audience gets to earn the ending of the film. The audience is going through the trials with the character. When Rocky wins (in *Rocky II*, etc.), the audience wins with him.

The director sets up the *Tension-then-Release Pattern.* From the opening moments of the film, the audience should be thirsty for a satisfying end. The audience wants to get what they expect AND more. They look for that special twist—that extra creativity. In The *Sixth Sense* (directed by M. Night Shyamalan), the big twist happened at the end . . . **Spoiler Alert** . . . when the audience discovers that the Bruce Willis character was dead already. This gives special meaning to Haley Joel Osment saying, "I see dead people."

How about the camera? Does the director use the placement of the camera to create audience satisfaction?

Yes. The placement of the camera is used to serve the story. Often in James Bond films, he is chased or he is doing the chasing. When Bond is chasing a villain, Bond usually races left to right which in Hollywood-type films is the direction that heroes use. To convey strength, directors use a low angle on the hero. For example, in a powerful fight scene in *Kung Fu Panda*, after the Furious Five defeat the villain Tai Lung (a snow leopard), the victorious team is filmed from a low angle to emphasize their strength and victory.

Section Three: Make the Screenplay Excellent
2. What the Director Needs to Know about Screenwriting:

What details do directors have to really know when it comes to screenplays?

Directors need to focus on the structure of a screenplay. Structure can help the director create an immediate connection with the audience. Structure relates to the *Conditioning of the Audience*. We, as audience members, have been conditioned to expect certain structures or patterns including:
- the big chase just before the end
- the final one-on-one fight between the hero and villain
- the betrayal
- the big twist at the end of the film

The Betrayal and the Big Twist combine in *Unbreakable* (written and directed by M. Night Shyamalan) when the Samuel L. Jackson character turns out to be the villain, although he had helped the Bruce Willis character earlier in the film.

You've talked about the audience's conditioning. But what about complaints about formula?

When I started teaching college level digital filmmaking, I coined the phrase (and developed a process) *The Cure for the Common Formula*. The "cure" arises from the specific details and a theme with emotional impact.

To encapsulate the ideas about the value of specific details, I coined the phrase: *Go through the tunnel of specific to get to the universal.*

Many filmmakers/screenwriters start in an upside down manner. They may say, "I want to write about 'man's inhumanity to man.'" Wait a minute. Let's talk about specifics. Not "man" but one human being, "Joseph" who, during his childhood, was severely beaten by bullies. Then he grows up with a "survivor" attitude and covers up deadly side effects of a drug his company is developing.

Now we have the basis for a film. We need specifics. Along these lines, Nicholas Meyer (director of *Star Trek II: The Wrath of Khan*) warned that avoiding the specific in favor of the universal is to end up with "cafeteria food."

So let's start with the specific. Earlier, I mentioned, "D.S.L." I use a series of questions for the character that I call "D.S.L." ("What would you Die for?" or "Stand for?" or "Live for?") For example, let's say I'm writing a screenplay about "Mark."

Here's how I may form a basic outline.

Step One: Personally, I might answer the third D.S.L. question "I would live for helping people as an educator."

Step Two: I can make Mark an educator—a public

speaking instructor who arrived early for his class.

Step Three: I start asking questions. What would he do? I'll have Mark gaze out the window of his classroom. What would be startling for him to see? An alien ship.

Step Four: Now, let's apply the specifics. Mark is an educator. How would an educator react to seeing an alien spacecraft? He probably reads a lot. Perhaps he'd be open to new ideas and new experiences? Is he especially curious?

Now, the screenplay is starting with specifics.

I can see how "D.S.L." can relate to deeper levels of the film. What about the theme of the film?

Here are themes that come up in science fiction and fantasy films:
- Humans create monsters through their arrogance (*Frankenstein, Deep Blue Sea, Godzilla, Alligator*).
- The hero must decide between personal happiness and benefits to humankind (for example in *The Dark Knight*, The Batman decides to take on the label of villain so that citizens of Gotham City will hold onto the ideals that Harvey Dent stood for—before Harvey fell from grace.).
- Human society will get worse, but one human being can find meaning by becoming better (stronger, more capable) and saving other humans (*Terminator, Terminator II*).

Theme also relates to these details:
- The Hero's Struggle Against Societal Forces
- The Hero's Clinging to Misconceptions
- The Hero's Character Arc
- The Resolution at the End of the Film

What about the Resolution at the end of a film?

An author's final statement about a story's theme is often shown in the resolution at the end of the film. *Spirited Away* (written and directed by Hayao Miyazaki) begins with a distraught little girl, Chihiro, who whines about having to move away from her close friend. Through the story, Chihiro learns to work hard and make tough decisions. By the end of the film, she is well on her way to being a self-reliant, proactive decision maker.

Some themes in a film may not be reflected in the resolution of that film. But the themes can still resonate. For example, one scene I always remember from *Spirited Away* was when Chihiro gathered other team members at the bathhouse to pull together and remove junk (including a twisted bicycle) out of a river spirit's physical form. The idea of people gathering together to clean up the environment has been powerfully depicted in Spirited Away.

Do people usually remember the theme of a film?

Often. It is often part of the answer to "What is the movie about?" The audience members care about who the movie is about. We also need to focus on compelling characters. When people remember a film, they tend to remember a character and a line of dialogue:

- Why does it always have to be snakes? (Indiana Jones, *Raiders of the Lost Ark*)
- I am and always shall be your friend. (Spock, *Star Trek II: The Wrath of Khan*).
- Lois Lane: "Who are you?" Superman replies: "A friend." (*Superman, the Movie*)

How else does a director cure the Common Formula?

You turn a cliché on its head. For example, in one of my feature films, I turned around the cliché of someone stepping on a rake and knocking themselves out with the rake handle.

To turn around the cliché, I had the character, "Son," inadvertently step on the rake. But Son's lighting reflexes allow him to do a karate chop and *break the rake in half*. So he doesn't get hurt. But then you need to *close the loop*. That means, you still need to fulfill the subconscious expectation that someone must get hurt by the rake. The idea is to satisfy the audience but not in the way that they expect.

So a moment later, Son's friend, John, steps on the rake, but he does not get hit in the head. Remember, the rake is now half as tall. Ouch!

Is there something else that you teach your students and clients about structure?

If the director feels stuck, he or she can use "bookends" to structure a story in an audience-pleasing way. A bookend is the process of using an element that's repeated in a similar way at the end of the film. For example, if a film begins with a kid getting beaten by a hoodlum at a basketball court, the ending will likely include a return to that basketball court.

Effective writers also seek to place an additional, special twist to the bookend at the end of a film. How? One way is to take the first idea that pops in one's mind and turn it upside down. One example that jumps in my mind is the ending of the first *Rocky* film of the series. It seems there is only one choice: Rocky either wins or loses the fight. Instead, the *Rocky* film has an original ending . . . **Spoiler Alert** . . . he loses the fight by a split decision, but he has won in his own heart because he has "gone the distance"—lasted the fifteen rounds. Besides, he hugs his girlfriend. He is a winner in that he has a true loving relationship.

How about lines of dialogue that are repeated in a film?

This is called an *echo* which ties into the audience's delight at experiencing something that recurs. In *Titanic*, the echo was "You jump, I jump—remember?"

In *Avatar*, the phrase "I see you" is repeated at various points in the film. The phrase forms the heart of the movie's song, "I See You," sung by Leona Lewis.

Near the end of *Avatar*, the female lead character, Neytiri, sees for the first time Jake's human form as he's gasping in the planet's atmosphere. Neytiri gets him a breathing unit and cradles Jake's alien (to her) form because she has "seen" his soul. He is truly a beautiful soul and she sees beyond his frail, alien body. As Jake regains consciousness, he says to Neytiri, "I see you"—the traditional Na'vi greeting meaning "I see who you truly are."

At the end of the film, Jake, now permanently one with his Na'vi body, opens his eyes. He now permanently sees life and the universe with the view of the Na'vi. He has found his people and his home.

Would you share something about structure related to comedy?

Sure. Let's face it: audiences love viewing a villain's comeuppance. In comedy, the audience laughs vigorously when an arrogant character slips and falls. We tend to enjoy the depiction of *pride goeth before a fall*.

Section Three: Make the Screenplay Excellent

3. What the Director Needs to Know about Creating Compelling Characters:

Is there some short cut for the director and screenwriter to add depth to a character?

In 1999, I came up with a short cut to identifying a character's values. I called it, "D.S.L."

As a side note: I combined an idea gleaned from the 1991 movie *Robin Hood: Prince of Thieves* and the catchy technology term DSL (introduced in 1998).

The first question I focused on was "What would you Die for?" because I recalled the lyric of "I would die for you" from the love song of *Robin Hood: Prince of Thieves*.

So my process includes asking these three questions:

- What would you Die for?
- What would you Stand for?
- What would you Live for?

Hence, my short cut is called "D.S.L."

The question of "live for?" arose when I thought about how tough it is to live for someone. For example, I know an engineer who had to become a stay-at-home nurse for his dying mother. He had to learn a number of skills to try to keep his mother as comfortable as possible and to maintain her life. To watch someone you love wither and die must be more painful than the momentary "heroic death" we see characters endure in films.

Is there a pitfall in how a character makes an "entrance" into a feature film?

Yes! The pitfall is to have a faulty introduction of a character. The effective director must fascinate the audience with the correct first impression of a character. The director wants the audience to care about the hero—and often, to revile the villain. It all begins the character's "entrance."

For example, Tai Lung, a snow leopard and villain of *Kung Fu Panda*, had a powerful "entrance." In breaking out of jail, Tai Lung demonstrated ferocious martial arts skill as he kicked and punched his way through at least twenty guards.

The entrance of a character is crucial. You create the audience's first impression, which lasts through the whole film. The pitfall is introducing a character as "cold" or unappealing and the film never recovers. For example, viewers of the film *Captains Courageous* have told me that they found the boy character to be a "brat" and they did not care when he grew into maturity under the tutelage of his mentor, Manuel (portrayed by Spencer Tracy). In essence, the audience members had "written off the character."

I was concerned that my films would get audiences to care about the main characters. Realizing that audiences harshly judge characters as they're introduced, I came up with the idea I call *Character as Acquaintance (CAA)*. It was 2000, and I shared with my college students that, in essence, a character, to an audience member, is like an acquaintance and *not* a friend. Writers spend so much time with their characters that they become like friends. With friends, we grant more leeway because we know their various sides. On the other hand, with strangers and acquaintances, we tend to quickly make judgments to guard our own feelings.

Good writers remember that audiences are quick to judge characters in the first seconds of their initial appearance.

The director must introduce a main character by focusing on:
- talent
- skills
- closeness (the audience connects with the character or the character is close with another character . . . even a pet cat)
- competence

In *Raiders of the Lost Ark,* Indiana Jones has one of the best entrances of a main character. Jones marches through the jungle, his two unsavory followers trailing behind him. He's definitely the man in charge. One of his followers pulls a gun and almost magically Jones swings around, snaps his whip and disarms the assailant. The guy runs off. Only then do we see Indiana Jones' face. Tough. Masculine. Powerful. In addition, Jones demonstrates talent (almost a sixth sense), skills and competence.

Often, heroes are introduced in the Ordinary World (a term from author Joseph Campbell, who wrote about the "hero's journey.") The Ordinary World tends to be a dull, stifling home or work situation. For example, near the beginning of *The Incredibles,* former superhero Bob Parr is stuck in a dead-end job at an insurance agency. He longs to return to his former life as a superhero, saving people. But he is stuck in the "Supers Relocation Program" that the government has set up so that superheroes are decommissioned and forced to hide. The superheroes had done good work but the collateral damage to property created multi-million dollar lawsuits.

The audience waits with great anticipation for Bob to break free and take up being a superhero again.

How does the director make compelling characters?

In his book, *A Hero with a Thousand Faces*, Joseph Campbell identified the archetypes of myths around the world. Archetype is defined as "An original model or type after which other similar things are patterned." Joseph Campbell identified the following archetypical characters: young hero, mentor, trickster, tempter/temptress and villain/antagonist.

a. Young hero. A prime example of the young hero is Luke in *Star Wars: Episode IV - A New Hope*. Luke is a farm boy who is trained by his mentor, Obi wan Kenobi, to harness the power of the Force so that he can face Darth Vader and other members of the evil Empire.

b. Mentor. This is the teacher who guides the young hero toward new skills and insights. For example, in *The Matrix*, the hero, Neo, is guided by his mentor, Morpheus, to perform super-human feats inside the Matrix or false world.

c. Trickster. The trickster conducts pranks on the main character. For example, in *Star Wars: Episode V: The Empire Strikes Back*, Yoda first appears to Luke Skywalker as a goofy, little creature. To learn if Luke is a worthy apprentice, Yoda tricks Luke. Yoda discovers that Luke is a good, kind person. Then, Yoda assumes his role as the Mentor.

d. Tempter/temptress. In *Indiana Jones and the Last Crusade*, Indiana Jones and his father, Dr. Henry Jones, Sr., have romantic encounters with Elsa, who secretly works for the Nazis. Dr. Henry Jones, Sr. (portrayed by Sean Connery), says, "[I slept with Elsa, but] I didn't trust her. Why did you?" Often, the temptress seeks to derail the hero from continuing to pursue his quest. Often, the temptress betrays the hero during the course of the story.

e. Villain/Antagonist. The hero must overcome the resistance that the villain provides. Villains often have an opposite philosophy to the hero's philosophy. For example, a villain believes in ego and selfish gain, while a hero believes in protecting the innocent. Heroes must become stronger when facing a tough villain. It takes seven films before Harry Potter is strong enough to face the villain Voldemort. In their own minds, villains see themselves as "the hero" and they feel justified to take what they want—and toss people around like pawns in a chess game.

Is there another way to make a compelling character?

The director must ensure that the character has clear values and goals. Feature films must present characters, plots and ideas with great economy. Every word of dialogue must be directed toward the through-line. The through-line is often called the spine of the story. In human anatomy the backbone holds the person erect, and the spine of the story is the crucial framework of the story.

Audiences must be given the character's clear values and goals early in the story or they will feel lost. Walt Disney said, "The audience needs to have a rooting interest." This means that the audience needs to know what the character wants in order to root for the character to get what she wants. For example, in the film *Legally Blonde,* a blonde sorority queen (portrayed by Reece Witherspoon) is dumped by her boyfriend. She's also put down as being shallow and unintelligent. We see her feelings devastated. So we root for her when she does not give up and follows her boyfriend to law school to get him back. We cheer when she demonstrates her abilities and legal savvy—and reclaims her dignity.

What about a character that makes no sense?

To counteract this problem, the director must ensure that there is consistency in character. Consistency in character is demonstrated when a character shows a seed of a trait at the beginning of the film, and the trait comes to full fruition at the end of the film. For example, in the extended cut of *Avatar*, Jake Sully's legs are paralyzed and he is stuck in a wheelchair. But when he sees a young woman mistreated by a hoodlum, Jake still rushes to her aid. Jake demonstrates courage and also gallant values. Later, he consistently demonstrates these traits on the alien planet when he battles creatures, meets Neytiri, and goes through death-defying training. Jake does not hesitate to jump astride a creature that resembles a flying dragon.

What is another way to have the audience connect with the character?

Have the audience experience a form of resolution with the character. I remember talking with my own father about *Field of Dreams*. He asked, "Isn't that a movie about baseball?" I explained to him that baseball is just a tip of the iceberg.

Actually, *Field of Dreams* moves many men to cry (including me—yes, I admit it) because Ray (portrayed by Kevin Costner) gets to experience some resolution with his father.

At first, the powerful resolution of *Field of Dreams* did not work. A test audience questioned if Ray and his father truly understood that through a miracle they were "sharing a catch." Something was missing. One word: "Dad."

In the revision, as his father starts to walk away, we hear

the word, "Dad?" And Ray's father, in ghostly form, turns around. Ray asks, "Do you want to have a catch?" They play catch and that's when the tears fall for many men.

This is one simple revision that celebrates how a test audience can be truly helpful.

Section Three: Make the Screenplay Excellent

4. What A Director Need to Know About Focus and Clarity for the Film:

Is there a short cut for the director to have a solid focus for the film?

Yes. One can focus on one idea. For *Back to the Future*, co-writer Bob Gale began with one experience. He found his father's high school yearbook and saw that his father had been class president. Gale later said, "I had nothing to do with the president of my high school class. . . . I wondered if I would have been my father's friend."

For the film *Tootsie*, the central idea was: "A man becomes a better man by portraying a woman."

Good directors work to boil down a screenplay to one powerful idea. For example, Francis Ford Coppola boiled down one of his films to the word obsession.

Shouldn't everything in a film be leading in one direction?

That would be the spine of the story — also known as the through line. In the *Harry Potter* series of eight films, everything leads toward Harry facing the evil Voldemort. Numerous characters sacrifice so much (some give their own lives) to keep Harry alive until he becomes strong enough and mature enough to face an overwhelming opponent.

On the way toward the final confrontation, Harry endures a number of "reversals." A reversal is a moment when a situation goes from good to horribly bad.

For example, in the final film of the franchise *Harry Potter and The Deathly Hallows, Part 2*, Harry sees that his beloved professor Remus Lupin and his wife have died in the battle. Harry knows that he must now end the conflict to avoid any more deaths of his beloved friends and supporters.

So for focus and clarity in the film, the director needs to ask: where is the Dark Moment? Where is the reversal? Is there a second reversal?

Section Three: Make the Screenplay Excellent

5. What a Director Needs to Know About a Great Beginning for a Feature Film:

How can the director make quick adjustments to make the beginning of a film compelling?

I suggest using what I call the *Three Elements of a Great Beginning*:
- startling image
- dramatic question
- "salting phrases"

A *Startling Image* is something that seizes the attention of the audience. For example, in the film Moonraker, James Bond is tossed out of a plane, but he has no parachute! The audience cheered when Bond chased after the villain in efforts to get his parachute. Bond adjusted his body to a streamlined form so he could race through the air toward the villain.

A *Dramatic Question* arises in the audience's mind on

viewing the opening scene. For one of my films, I began with a character whose face hits the pavement. Questions arise for the audience: Is he dead? Was he shot? Who shot him? Will the hero see justice is served?

Salting phrases are often dialogue that create curiosity. This is based on the idea "You can lead a horse to water but you can't make him drink"—unless you salt his oats first. With salt one makes the audience thirsty for more. For example, a sci-fi film noir movie could begin with a narration by the main character: "If I knew what trouble she'd bring, I would have told my heart to shut up and taken a shuttle to Saturn. No. I would have shot her, taken the shuttle. My heart would've been just fine."

To improve your film, you could use one or all three of the above elements.

In *Section Four, Develop the Film Project,* we will cover elements of structure that a director can emphasize to lead team members to improve the film.

SECTION FOUR: DEVELOP THE FILM PROJECT

6. What a Director Needs to Know About "Hollywood-type" Films and Buddy Films:

Tell me about the structure of Buddy Films.

I have identified Four Elements of a Buddy Film:
- the "buddies don't like each other" scene
- a bonding scene
- a dark moment in which the buddies appear to split up
- a rescue of one buddy by the other one

An initial scene in which buddies dislike each other occurs when the buddies express differences, perhaps, in taste, culture and habits. At the beginning of the film *Rush Hour*, the Jackie Chan character and Chris Tucker character do not get along. At one point, Jackie Chan turns on Chris' car radio. In response to the music, Jackie exclaims: "Beach

Boys. Great American Music." Chris retorts: "Don't you ever touch a black man's radio, boy! You can do that in China but you can get your ass killed out here, man!"

The bonding scene often occurs when two heroes pause a moment and make a personal connection. Often, one buddy reveals a personal detail or secret; or, one buddy demonstrates a special understanding about the other one's approach to life.

Here is an example that I've written as an illustration. Two officers from separate planets and conflicting cultures are assigned to track down a killer and save a little girl. They are pinned down with gunfire:

"Another day at the office," Kerrin says.
Schretan grunts.
"What led you to joining the Shield?"
"Nothing much," Schretan says.
"What was her name?" Kerrin asks.
"What?" Schretan asks.
"Sarah dumped me so I—"
"Mindy," Schretan replies, "My sister was kidnapped and . . ."

So these lines of dialogue provide a start to a bonding scene in which the characters ultimately discover that they share an urgent need to see justice dispensed.

Section Four: Develop the Film Project
7. What a Director Needs to Know About Having Depth in the Film:

Isn't it important to have a film that gets people to talk about it?

Yes. I call this coffee shop talk, which occurs when audience members talk about a film after viewing it.

For example, my friends still talked about *Inception*—for months afterward. . . . **Spoiler Alert** . . . At the end of the film, the audience is left with a number of questions including: Did the Leonardo DiCaprio character make it back to reality? Or was his "happy ending" actually part of a dream? Director-writer Christopher Nolan left it up in the air. As a screenwriter, I knew what the last shot would be when I saw the spinning top totem. The totem was supposed to help the operative know whether he or she was still in a dream. I quickly surmised that a spinning top would be in the last shot. And so it was.

What other details give a film some texture?

Multiple layers to a film can arise from the values of your characters. Values can include: loyalty, love, creativity, freedom, material abundance, compassion, courage and more. Some directors really connect with certain material because in some way a director's values are mirrored in the hero's goals.

Other layers of the film can relate to the cultural context. A culture includes shared beliefs about spirituality, human rights, values, languages, gender roles and more.

Then there are the filmmakers' underlying beliefs. How the characters interact and how the story is resolved reflects the underlying beliefs of the director. For example in the *Harry Potter* series, Hermione frequently saves her two male companions because she's smarter and better at magic than they are.

Tell me about details related to the hero.

The hero has a clear and fervent purpose. Without a purpose, the audience does not know what to root for. With no goal or purpose, the audience does not know when the hero is winning. It often helps to have a sidekick character so that we do not laugh at the hero. It is best to separate the functions of characters to keep things clear. It is hard to cry with a character if you laughed at him in the previous scene.

Many screenwriters have studied Joseph Campbell's "hero's journey." In many stories that follow the hero's journey pattern, the hero meets a mentor. For example, in *Finding Nemo*, Marlin, the father-character, meets "Crush," a sea turtle. As a temporary mentor, Crush teaches Marlin about how it's necessary to let go and allow one's children to explore and grow up. Crush's message is one of the important things that Marlin learns through the journey of the story.

Section Four: Develop the Film Project

8. What a Director Needs to Know About Making a Fantasy Film:

Tell me about the specifics of making a fantasy film.

Let me begin by showing similarities in two sagas of the science fantasy genre: *The Matrix Saga* and *The Star Wars Saga*.

It is interesting to note:
- both have mentors (Morpheus, Oracle, Obi-wan)
- both have a young hero (Neo, Luke, Anakin) with supernatural powers
- both follow the story of the Chosen One

- both have a Quest
- both use redemption as a theme

How about the spine of a fantasy film?

Fantasy films often focus on a young hero who must learn something. As the hero learns, the audience also vicariously learns. When the hero triumphs at the end, the audience has also vicariously earned the reward. What reward? It varies. The hero earns true love. The hero discovers hidden virtue she didn't know she had. It can be tangible: the hero wrestles the kingdom back from the villain. Sometimes, it's really obvious (some say, "too obvious"), at the end of *Star Wars: Episode IV: A New Hope,* Luke and Han are actually given medals! The spine of a fantasy film often centers on a quest. When the hero has gained some object that helps him or her vanquish evil and set the world aright—then the film is over.

Tell me about the creation of a world.

William Gibson, creator of the word cyberspace and author of the story and screenplay *Johnny Mnemonic* and the novel *Neuromancer*, told me, "It is absolutely essential to establish the parameters of possibility. While you're writing, you may run into something that resets the parameters. And then you go back and fill it in." The fantasy screenwriter must often explain how magic powers function in the world of his or her script.

It seems that in fantasy films there are stock characters.

Stock characters include a young hero who usually meets allies, a mentor and of course, a villain. Kurt Wimmer, the director/writer of *Equilibrium*, told me how he emphasizes conflict as the central element of every story. (This is echoed by my screenwriting mentors.) In Hollywood-type films, the conflict revolves around the hero's battle with a villain. The hero must meet resistance in order to complete his or her goals. In fantasy films, the villain or antagonist is usually an incredibly powerful wizard, sorcerer, sorceress, or magician. Only through facing resistance and struggling through conflict can the hero grow and learn. A strong villain requires the hero to demonstrate courage, persistence, and resourcefulness.

Is there something that really grabs you about fantasy films?

In a number of interviews, celebrated author Ray Bradbury emphasizes fantasy's ability to move the reader's heart.

Love is the answer to everything. It's the only reason to do anything. If you don't write stories you love, you'll never make it. If you don't write stories that other people love, you'll never make it. - Ray Bradbury

Fantasy films often provide something I enjoy: heightened reality. Heightened reality describes the use of fantastic elements in order to give the audience a profound emotional experience.

For example, there is a profound moment in the film *Crouching Tiger, Hidden Dragon*. The Chow Yun-Fat character tells his love, the Michelle Yeoh character, "I have one last breath." She implores him to use it to ensure his transition to heaven. Instead, he decides to tell her of his love. He says, "I would rather be a ghost, drifting by your side...as a condemned soul...than enter heaven without you. Because of your love...I will never be a lonely spirit."

What a powerful moment for people who have been deeply in love. Since we're talking about ghosts and the afterlife, a number of people relegate *Crouching Tiger, Hidden Dragon* to the genre of fantasy. The declaration of love is an example of "heightened reality" in that in the fantasy setting we see there is no deeper level of love—to risk one's soul.

It's not often that such an intense idea about love can be expressed in film or literature.

Aren't there timeless themes in fantasy films?

Yes. Timeless themes include:
- love
- loyalty
- a cause worth fighting for (perhaps, freedom or preserving the lives of loved ones)

About *The Lord of the Rings Trilogy* and author J.R.R. Tolkien, director Peter Jackson said, "I think [Lord of the Rings] is timeless. . . . All the themes Tolkien wrote about, it was stuff that he was passionate about. . . . He was ahead of his time in some cases. His love of the English countryside, and his hatred of factories, and his hatred of chopping the forests down to fuel the engines of industry. . . . other themes of his were much more broad—the themes of friendship, and war, and the fact that… some wars are worth fighting. What Tolkien was certainly saying is that what is worth fighting is enslavement. If people are trying to enslave you, then you should stand up against them and fight back. And, yet, he also very clearly was making a point that when you win that war, that you don't really win. There are no ultimate winners in war; there are only people that lose. You come out of war changed, and no matter the justness of the war, you come home different. That's obviously very much true of Frodo. He didn't win; he lost. He lost who he was. He lost his sense of innocence. Even though what he did was justified."

How does the director make a fantasy film grab the audience?

The director takes great care with creating the world. Why? The director must guide the audience to the point of a willing suspension of disbelief.

Director Peter Jackson said, "We set ourselves the job of making more of an historical than a fantasy film [The Lord of the Rings], because I just thought that would be interesting, to treat fantasy as history, as if it had a degree of reality to it. So everything we did in the movie we tried to make feel real and just tried to avoid an over-designed sort of film and tried to make it more earthy and organic."

To grab the audience, the filmmaker must establish early on that the film portrays a fantastic world. This world has its internal logic, so the audience members must suspend their disbelief and let go of the reflexive response, "Oh, that's not possible."

For example, near the beginning of *Labyrinth*, director Jim Henson establishes that the young girl, Sarah, has an appreciation for fairy tales. Then, in the next scene, Sarah's father and her step mother prepare to leave to go out on the town, but they force Sarah to care for her step baby brother. With the adults gone, the baby starts crying loudly. Sarah recites a tale to the crying child:

"Once upon a time, there was a beautiful young girl whose stepmother always made her stay home with the baby. And the baby was a spoiled child, and wanted everything to himself, and the young girl was practically a slave. But what no one knew is that the king of the goblins had fallen in love with the girl, and he had given her certain powers. So one night, when the baby had been particularly cruel to her, she called on the goblins for help!"

Suddenly, the goblins in Sarah's closet all open their eyes as one exclaims: "Listen!"

Sarah continues reciting her tale to the baby: "'Say your right words,' the goblins said, 'and we'll take the baby to the castle, and you will be free!' But the girl knew that the Goblin King would keep the baby in his castle for ever and ever and ever, and turn it into a goblin! And so the girl suffered in silence. Until one day, when she was tired from a day of housework, and she was hurt by the harsh words of her stepmother, and she could no longer stand it . . ."

The baby boy continues his infernal crying.

Sarah continues reciting: "I can bear it no longer! Goblin King! Goblin King! Wherever you may be take this child of mine far away from me!"

Still in Sarah's closet, a goblin says: "That's not it! Where did she get that rubbish? It doesn't even start with 'I wish!'"

Soon Sarah states the curse correctly and the story is off and running.

The creepy moment of the goblins opening their eyes is startling and we know that we're in an extraordinary tale. The director has the task of seizing the audience's attention. I often call this "The Cool Factor," a term that I coined. I'm describing the moment of a film during which audience members say, "Oh! That's cool!"

Are there important decisions about who functions as the narrator?

Yes. Some fantasy films/TV series begin with an anonymous narrator. One example that works well is Jim Dale as the narrator of the TV series *Pushing Daisies*. He provides just the right tone that comes across as a little twisted and kind of amused.

On the other hand, having a character function as narrator can create more connection for the audience. If the main character is the narrator, we get to feel their feelings. A prime example is acerbic narration of Dexter in the *Dexter* TV series.

I notice that a number of fantasy and science fiction stories begin with a written introduction. Would you share your thoughts on that?

A written introduction quickly provides the back-story, which includes events that preceded the beginning of the film. For example, the written introduction for one of the cuts of the film *Blade Runner* includes:

> "Early in the 21st Century, the Tyrell Corporation advanced Robot evolution in the Nexus phase—a being virtually identical to a human—known as a Replicant.
>
> The Nexus 6 Replicants were superior in strength and agility, and at least equal in intelligence, to the genetic engineers who created them.
>
> Replicants were used Off-world as slave labor, in the hazardous exploration and colonization of other planets.
>
> After a bloody mutiny by a Nexus 6 combat team in an Off-world colony, Replicants were declared illegal on

earth—under penalty of death.

Special police squads—Blade Runner Units—had orders to shoot to kill, upon detection, any trespassing Replicant.

This was not called execution.

It was called retirement."

I must admit that I prefer the narrated introduction of *The Lord of the Rings* that had many stunning visuals to convey back-story.

What do you recommend a director place special effort on?

It's crucial to have an "opening fantastic image." Some directors like to have the first image be startling. For example, a director could choose to open her film with a shot of a castle at night with lightning flashing and a dragon landing on one of the castle's spires. Other directors provide a startling image after a few shots. For example, *The Matrix* was released in 1999, but people still remember the amazing shot of Trinity leaping into the air as she does a flying kick. At that instant, the camera move is an amazing 360-degree shot of her.

What about an archetypal character?

As I mentioned elsewhere in this book, many screenwriters study Joseph Campbell's "hero's journey" in which Campbell describes archetypical characters like the young hero, mentor and others. Another recognizable character is the underdog, and in recent years, audiences have been treated to the essential underdog character Harry Potter. Just like Cinderella, he grows up under the thumb of cruel relatives.

Even a highly trained, skilled character can begin as an

underdog. For example, the main character Jason Bourne of *The Bourne Identity* is introduced as barely alive, having been shot and adrift in the ocean. Through much of the film he desperately tries to stay alive while being hunted—and still hoping to recover his memory.

* * * * * *

Section Four: Develop the Film Project

9. What a Director Needs to Know About Making the Horror Film:

What would help a director make a better horror film?

Stephen King wrote a celebrated article entitled "Why We Crave Horror Movies." Here is a portion of that article:

"But anticivilization emotions don't go away, and they demand periodic exercise. . . . If we share a brotherhood of man, then we also share an insanity of man. None of which is intended as a defense of either the sick joke or insanity but merely as an explanation of why the best horror films, like the best fairy tales, manage to be reactionary, anarchistic, and revolutionary all at the same time.

The mythic horror movie, like the sick joke, has a dirty job to do. It deliberately appeals to all that is worst in us. It is morbidity unchained, our most base instincts let free, our nastiest fantasies realized . . . and it all happens, fittingly enough, in the dark. . . . For myself, I like to see the most aggressive of them—*Dawn of the Dead*, for instance—as lifting a trap door in the civilized forebrain and throwing a basket of raw meat to the hungry alligators swimming around in that subterranean river beneath.

Why bother? Because it keeps them from getting out, man. It keeps them down there and me up here. It was Lennon and McCartney who said that all you need is love, and I would agree with that.

As long as you keep the gators fed."

On other occasions, King said, "We make up horrors to help us cope with the real ones." And, "Monsters are real, and ghosts are real too. They live inside us, and sometimes, they win."

Although he acknowledges human failings, King does have characters who do the right thing. So we can find some inspiration in his stories. King said, "It's better to be good than evil, but one achieves goodness at a terrific cost."

So how does a director make a better horror film? To answer this question let's also view what another horror novelist, Dean Koontz, has written: "Suspense in fiction results primarily from the reader's identification with and concern about lead characters who are complex, convincing, and appealing."

So the effective director makes sure the screenplay has characters that audience members care about. Many directors keep encouraging the screenwriter to make improvements to a script to bring out the elements that audience members can identify with. Dean Koontz wrote: "I believe that we carry within us a divinely inspired moral imperative to love, and I explore that imperative in all of my books...We have within us the ability to change for the better and to find dignity as individuals rather than as fragments of one mass movement or another."

Along these lines, Stephen King said, "You have got to love the people ... that allows horror to be possible."

One of my favorite films of all time is *Jaws*. I truly care about the characters and I find the film to be in large part a character study. The film had to be; the darn mechanical shark wouldn't work. Certainly, the good man, Chief Brody, seeks redemption after he allowed himself to be bullied by town officials to keep the beach open for swimming. After a boy is torn apart by a shark, Chief Brody charters a boat to hunt down the shark—even though Brody is terrified of the water and drowning.

What about horror and suspense?

Ask a number of people what horror means to them and they may mention grisly images of blood and severed body parts. They will probably talk of stock characters of the horror genre: vampires, ghosts, serial killers, demons, and others.

Still, horror involves primal fears related to survival and physical pain. Horror is also visceral—that is, instinctive or deeply emotional. In addition, Dean Koontz said, "Believable characters are what hold a horror story together. They are the engines of its power . . . Every book [I write] has some real life in it. I was never pursued by an evil twin clone, but everything else in Mr. Murder was pretty much out of my own life."

Suspense is the experience of anticipation—often, that something bad is about to occur. Alfred Hitchcock, the director of *Psycho* and *Vertigo*, expressed his preference for suspense over merely getting audience members to be startled or shocked. Hitchcock talked about creating suspense by alerting the audience to a bomb ticking away underneath a card table surrounded by oblivious people. Hitchcock was opposed to suddenly having an explosion and just getting a startling effect. He definitely preferred the creation of suspense.

How can the director increase the horror?

An effective way to increase horror is to place it in the *Context of an Everyday Experience*.

Stephen King's book (and mini-series), *Bag of Bones*, begins with the horror of the death of a loved one. The main character's wife dies after being hit by a speeding bus. I felt empathy for the main character and I continued watching the mini-series.

Steven Spielberg's *Poltergeist* (directed by Tobe Hooper) focused on ghostly attacks upon a family in the suburbs.

Many people feel trapped by everyday circumstances. Stephen King translated his own fear of being forced to write something he couldn't stand into a dilemma facing an author in the novel *Misery*.

It's reported that King wrote the novel as a reaction to what happened in his own life. A deranged fan broke into King's home, held King's wife hostage in their home, and claimed that King had taken the fan's manuscript.

In *Misery*, Stephen King intensifies the situation by creating a serial killer/deranged fan character named Annie Wilkes. She imprisons and maims an author named Paul Sheldon. The novel (and film) *Misery* accesses our fears related to slavery, imprisonment, and being at the mercy of an insane killer.

Both King and Koontz emphasize that the readers/audience must care for the protagonists. And in *Misery*, Paul Sheldon demonstrates resourcefulness and courage in order to free himself of assailant Annie Wilkes.

Section Four: Develop the Film Project
10. What the Director Needs to Know About "Fairy Tale Elements" in Modern Feature Films:

Are there fairy tale elements in mainstream films?

Yes. Three elements come to mind: 1) the Damsel in Distress, 2) the Lone Knight, and 3) One True Love.

Let's begin with the *Damsel in Distress*, which appears in many films. In recent films, we see women fighting back and I, for one, applaud that. For example, in *Spider-Man*, Mary Jane Watson defends herself in an intense struggle. Alas, there are too many hoodlums and Spider-Man must come to her rescue. In *Die Another Day*, the last film in which Pierce Brosnan starred as James Bond, Halle Berry portrays a savvy and athletic spy herself. In the finale, two fights take place: Bond vs. the lead villain and the Halle Berry-character vs. a female villain.

Isn't the hero often alone?

Yes. This is The Lone Knight. I'm reminded of *Shane*, in which a gunfighter comes to town, dispatches the villains and, although shot, leaves a family in peace. With the boy yelling, "Come back, Shane!"

Tom Cruise portrayed Jack Reacher, the main character in a series of Lee Child novels. The first film is entitled *Jack Reacher* and it features Jack, who comes to town, sets things right, has a brief romance, and moves on to the next adventure. Jack Reacher usually only carries the clothes he's wearing and a toothbrush. Along the way, he usually secures a firearm to defend himself.

Both *Spider-Man* (staring Toby McGuire) and *Superman II* (staring Christopher Reeve) end with the hero going it alone. The hero must not have a romantic partner because villains can use her against him. The lone hero is supposed to put his mission or quest above personal happiness.

What about the love relationships?

Hollywood-style feature films emphasize *One True Love*. In real life, a number of people find love after widowhood, perhaps, in a second marriage. But Hollywood-style films, particularly romantic comedies, set up that the hero (or heroine) is in the wrong relationship (and it's really obvious!). Then, through the course of the film, the main character eventually wins the heart of his or her true love.

Some fans of romantic comedies point to the following lines of dialogue from *Pretty Woman*:

Richard Gere-character: "So what happened after he [the knight] climbed up the tower and rescued her?"

Julia Roberts-character: "She rescued him right back."

More recently, some female characters demonstrate that they can be a knight in their own lives. They can, with healthy self-esteem, create personal fulfillment. Films like *Living Out Loud* end with the woman walking alone, as a self-sufficient individual who does not need a romantic partner to feel complete.

Section Four: Develop the Film Project

11. What a Director Needs to Know About Making a Science Fiction Film:

What distinguishes a science fiction film from a fantasy film?

In science fiction, the important word is *extrapolation*. Dictionary.com defines extrapolation as "to infer or estimate by extending or projecting known information."

Science fiction usually focuses on staying within the laws of physics. For example, Steven Spielberg gathered a group of futurists to help him enhance *Minority Report*. Spielberg wanted a think-tank to discuss what advanced technology might be present 30 years beyond the production of the film. The thinkers came up with the idea that advertisements will be triggered by a person's eyes—the unique retina patterns

Extrapolation starts with what is and moves on to what could be. Currently advertisers seek any advantage to push their products. If advertisers, like in a scene in *Minority Report*, could call your name to get you to look at a billboard, they would.

Spielberg's think-tank group devised the sick-stick which is a club a police officer uses to make a person vomit. The officer incapacitates the criminal with one touch.

Fantasy is a genre in which the author/filmmaker makes up her own rules. Sometimes, fantasy filmmakers look upon magic as a form of "technology" passed from mentor to apprentice. For example, in the TV series, *Merlin* (first broadcast on BBC One in 2008), the young Merlin is guided by his mentor Gaius.

Section Four: Develop the Film Project
12. What a Director Needs to Know About Parody, Satire and Comedy:

What about films with satire or parody?

We'll begin with definitions:
- Satire is a form of literature that uses wit, irony, or

sarcasm to discredit something, often in a humorous way.
- Parody is a form of literature in which something or someone is closely imitated for comic effect or ridicule.

A true comedy is often about foolish people without the likelihood that they will learn and grow. When I saw *The Hangover*, I did not feel that any character grew or matured. And that was confirmed with more mischief in *The Hangover II*.

Here's another example. The TV series *I Love Lucy* had a pattern. Lucy's husband Ricky would declare that he didn't want Lucy to be part of one of his shows, she would do some outlandish stunt—and somewhere along the line she would cry with a loud "Waaaaa!" So we did not see her character grow and mature.

Let's look at a main difference between satire and parody. Satire is often a serious examination of a topic, whereas parody is often void of a serious meaning. Stanley Kubrick's feature film, *Dr. Strangelove: Or How I learned to Love the Bomb* is a satire that explores a serious theme—the folly of humankind and the possibility of nuclear annihilation of the human species.

On the other hand, recent parodies entitled *Disaster Movie* and *Epic Movie* basically recreate scenes from popular movies like the *Chronicles of Narnia* or *Superman Returns*. These films fail to establish relatable characters or to engage the audience to care about the story or characters. The goal of parody is simply to ridicule something and gain laughs.

How can one add a bit of comedy to a film?

In *Seven Samurai*, director Akira Kurosawa created a terrific comedic moment. First, he sets up the situation in which a young man tests potential samurai (for a team) by hiding and then attacking the potential samurai with a large stick. All of the real, effective samurai easily evade the blow. Then the Toshiro Mifune-character saunters into the doorway. Akira Kurosawa cuts away, and we only hear the blow. Then we see Toshiro Mifune again, and he is rubbing his aching head. Audiences rock with laughter at this sight.

How can you add even more comedy?

The process is called "adding a button to a scene." For example, in *When Harry Met Sally*, director Rob Reiner added a button to the scene, that is, a big laugh to close the scene. In the film, the Meg Ryan-character simulates orgasm while talking with the Billy Crystal-character in a crowded diner. After Meg Ryan's display, a woman turns to a waiter and says, "I'll have what she's having." By the way, the actress with the last word was Rob Reiner's mother!

Section Four: Develop the Film Project
13. What the Director Needs to Know about Using a "Personal Style" and Standing Out from the Pack:

New film directors are concerned about developing a personal style. What are your thoughts on this?

One principle for a director can be "find yourself in the material."
Author Julia Cameron wrote: "Original means you are the origin of the work." For me, this means that when I direct a film and put myself into it I don't need to worry about it

being fresh. Also, I will make space for the actors and other team members to make interesting contributions to the film. The unique combination of our talents and efforts will elevate the film.

Earlier in this book, I wrote of the *D.S.L. questions*: What would you: Die for? Stand for? Live for? I mentioned that some directors connect personal values with some value that the main character holds.

The director can put her own deeply held convictions and beliefs into her work. Barbra Streisand (director of *Yentl*, *The Mirror Has Two Faces*) said, "Imagination and belief manifest reality." And from this idea, we realize that the effective director develops her own clarity and focus and then the cast and crew follow her "imagination and belief."

When directing *Raging Bull*, Martin Scorsese placed his personal knowledge of self-destruction into the depiction of the Robert DeNiro character. Then Scorsese added a "personal style" touch. Unlike other boxing films, Scorsese made a specific decision about the cinematography and had the camera enter the boxing ring and not exit the ring for shots of the audience. In essence, Scorsese gave more of a boxer's point of view.

Director-writer Quentin Tarantino (*Pulp Fiction*) is well-known for his unique style of dialogue. In *Kill Bill Part II*, Tarantino provided the following speech for the assassin Bill (portrayed by David Carradine). It's a dramatic moment because Bill drugged the heroine The Bride (portrayed by Uma Thurman). Bill could take his time and enjoy himself. He says:

"About two minutes [for the drug to take effect], just long enough for me to finish my point. Now, a staple of the superhero mythology is, there's the superhero and there's the alter ego.

Batman is actually Bruce Wayne, Spider-Man is actually Peter Parker. When that character wakes up in the morning, he's Peter Parker. He has to put on a costume to become Spider-Man. And it is in that characteristic Superman stands alone. Superman didn't become Superman. Superman was born Superman. When Superman wakes up in the morning, he's Superman. His alter ego is Clark Kent. His outfit with the big red 'S', that's the blanket he was wrapped in as a baby when the Kents found him. Those are his clothes. What Kent wears—the glasses, the business suit—that's the costume. That's the costume Superman wears to blend in with us. Clark Kent is how Superman views us. And what are the characteristics of Clark Kent. He's weak... he's unsure of himself... he's a coward. Clark Kent is Superman's critique on the whole human race."

With the rest of the dialogue, we, the audience, understand that Bill thinks that he and The Bride are the elite—the strong and superior people.

My point here is that Tarantino's gift with dialogue is part of his personal style. A lesser writer may have written, "You [The Bride] and I are special. Not like other people. They're weak."

It's up to each director to discover his or her own personal style—and to make the most of it.

What gives a film extra impact?

Focus on *What's the Worst That Can Happen?* I use a three-part structure that gives the following experience for the audience:
- Oh, no!
- Now what? and
- Oh, yes!

Oscar-winning screenwriter William Goldman said, "Give

the audience what they want—just not how they expect it."

That's what director-writer Josh Whedon did with *Serenity* (the science fiction feature film based on the TV series *Firefly*). At the one point, he began a sequence with a series of dark moments. Preacher, the mentor, dies. Another beloved character dies. Whedon said that he did that so that the audience would feel "anything can happen!"

That is the "Oh, no!" factor.

Two more characters are struck down, wounded, leaving one lone, thin teenage girl, River Tam, to stand up to about twenty Reavers (crazed, super strong, mutated humans). She jumps into a room with them and starts kicking and hacking at them with bladed weapons. Moments later, the doors are open and she is the lone one standing. She defeated them all. And the audience cheered. It was an "Oh, yes!" moment.

As a side note: we knew that River had been modified and programmed by the government. We just didn't know her special abilities were that powerful.

Section Four: Develop the Film Project

14. What a Director Needs to Know About Making a "Good Film"

What makes a good movie?

My first thought is vivid characters and a compelling story. Upon asking someone about a film that they like, you'll often hear details of character and dialogue:

- From *Goldfinger*:
James Bond: "Do you expect me to talk?"
Goldfinger: "No, Mr. Bond. I expect you to die."

- From *Raiders of the Lost Ark*:
Indiana Jones: "Why does it always have to be snakes?"

Elsewhere in the film:
Sallah: "What are you going to do, Indy?"
Indiana Jones: "I don't know. I'm making this up as I go along."

What makes a story compelling?

For years, in my graduate school classes, I have identified these elements that make a great story:
 a) Does the main character learn something?
 b) Does the main character gain a new skill that she/he uses at the end?
 c) Is the main character an underdog?
 d) Is the main character interesting? Talented? Skillful?
 e) Is a cliché turned "on its head"?
 f) Do characters come in and demonstrate loyalty and community? (like Han Solo's rescue of Luke at the end of *Star Wars IV: A New Hope*).
 g) Are there any "big ideas" in the story?

Numerous viewers consider the film *To Kill a Mockingbird* to be a classic work of cinema. Upon seeing the film, I felt inspired to distill the following assessment. A good movie . . .

- makes you really care about the characters
- surprises you
- makes you cry
- has moments that inspire laughter or smiles
- inspires you with human values to aspire to
- elicits your experience of suspense

In the extended cut of *Aliens*, Ripley (portrayed by Sigourney Weaver) lost a lifetime with her daughter. Ripley was trapped in suspended animation for around one hundred years and her daughter had already passed away by the time Ripley was awakened. So when she discovers a frightened little girl named Newt, Ripley takes on a heroic mission to be her mother-figure, who protects her from the alien creatures.

I mentioned "surprises you" as a key element of a good movie. How does the director surprise audience members? He or she avoids clichés. The answer is this: Get specific. You do that in two ways: a) find methods to make each character unique and b) avoid the standard patterns of screenwriting. For example, a usual war movie pattern is to have a lieutenant who is highly educated, refined and a poor leader of soldiers. Find some way to turn the cliché on its head. Instead, have the rough and tumble guy be the poor leader.

What about an intriguing premise?

The intriguing premise can begin with a question. For my book, *TimePulse: Beyond Titanic*, I started with the question: "What if a present day college instructor wakes up in an undersea city in which Titanic victims are alive and in the midst of a battle between two factions?"

One way to make something fresh and original is to flip the usual conventions.

For example, in the book series *The Age of Fire* by E.E. Knight, the stories are told from the point of the view of the dragon.

Shrek is told from the point of view of the ogre, when ogres are usually merely "cardboard" obstacles in the way of human adventurers.

Section Four: Develop the Film Project

15. What a Director Needs to Know About Working with "Experts" and Test Audience Members:

How can the director be careful to avoid being misled by test marketing or inappropriate guidance from so-called experts?

First, you need to observe carefully whether someone espousing an opinion has an inappropriate agenda or is simply not relevant to your particular film.

To gain true value from a critique, focus on these questions:
- Is the comment-maker in your target market?
- Is the comment-maker knowledgeable in the area of your focus?
- Is the comment-maker seeking to help you?
- Can the comment-maker help you compensate for your filmmaking tendencies?

Tell me about "tendencies."

A director may be an easygoing person so they may prefer a leisurely pace for the film. I'm the opposite. I tend to default to tight cutting of scenes. Because of this, I coined the phrase *"Know your tendencies and compensate for them."* To accomplish that, I tend to have a slow-pace editor view my rough cuts.

People tend to emulate what they like. Look at your private collection of films and you'll see what you like and what you'll probably emulate.

Sometimes, consulting an "expert" might provide the spark of a good idea. A test screening could also be helpful. For example, the makers of *Final Destination* ran a test screening, and discovered that they needed to add neutral footage after one character was abruptly run over by a bus. The filmmakers realized that the audience needed some time to catch their breath and finish with their nervous laughter.

How does the director stick to her original intentions in the face of criticism of her work?

One screenplay idea that surprised me was in the original script for *The Butterfly Effect*. The main character protected his friends by strangling himself with the umbilical cord while he was in the womb—so that he would not modify time and events. However, the studio decided to force a more conventional ending on the film.

The above is a prime example of what I call *homogenizing by committee*.

To make sure that your film is not watered down, be sure to write down your original intentions for your film. Then seek to get some form of useful responses from viewers of your rough cut.

You can ask:
a) Did this film elicit emotion in you? What emotion?
b) Did this film give you a new way to see a particular topic?
c) What was the best part of this film to you?

One year, I said to a colleague: "I'm not afraid of offending someone. I just want to know who." My point is that the most well-meaning film is likely to upset someone.

A filmmaker is often called on to be courageous. Because a film that tries to be all things to all people often turns out to be bland and formulaic—and it serves no one.

Can the film evolve into a new direction?

Yes. I remember that Orson Welles and Robert Altman talked about presiding over "happy accidents" on the set. Steven Spielberg does not like to hold real rehearsals because he wants to catch "lightning in a bottle."

The details of a film may change, but usually a director can hold to the original intention of the film. For example, Dustin Hoffman and director Sidney Pollack honed one line as the spine of *Tootsie*: "A man become a better man by portraying a woman." From that solid, simple point, the director and actors could discover new wrinkles and opportunities on the set. But the one line provided unity for the film.

SECTION FIVE: PREPRODUCTION

16. What a Director Needs to Know About Casting:

How can one deal with worries about casting?

James Cameron said, "I always go with my first impression; the audience does." His first impression of Leonardo DiCaprio was two-fold. First, DiCaprio did not want to audition for Titanic. Second, when DiCaprio finally came to Cameron's production offices, all of the female members of Cameron's production team office were missing. James Cameron eventually found the women in the conference room with Leo. That gave James an impression about Leo's magnetism.

Cameron went with his first impression instead of caving into the misgivings of the studio executives who were not impressed by DiCaprio's performance in dailies for the then in-production *Romeo + Juliet*.

An adage in filmmaking is: "Good casting means that your work is 90% done."

The Director's Guide to Casting:

Method #1: Pay attention and assess whether a potential actor is bitter or hard to work with.

Be sure to go to dinner or have coffee with the actor. See the actor when the person's "guard is down."

Method #2: Ask yourself: Has the actor devoted extra effort to prove he or she really wants the role?

Notice if the actor has already done some of the work. Here's a famous example. Elijah Wood wanted the part of Frodo in the *Lord of the Rings* series of motion pictures. With the help of a friend, Elijah made a videotape of himself in costume and using a British accent. When a casting person for director Peter Jackson saw the videotape, she said, "Peter, you must see this." Peter saw the tape and saw Elijah in a new light.

Here's another example: Audrey Meadows wanted the part of "Alice" in *The Honeymooners* TV show, for which Jackie Gleason functioned as producer and star. She came in for the interview. Jackie told his colleague, "She is too pretty. She is nothing like Alice." So Audrey got a photographer-friend to take photos of her in the kitchen with hair in disarray and in tattered clothes. Another friend brought the photos to Jackie, who said, "Who is this? She's Alice." The friend said, "That's Audrey Meadows, you already met her. . ." Jackie said, "Hire her."

Method #3: Ask yourself: Has the actor demonstrated

initiative? How much dedication does the actor have to this profession?

Actor Vin Diesel demonstrated his initiative and acting skills by casting himself and making his own feature film *Strays*. When Steven Spielberg saw the film, he cast Diesel in *Saving Private Ryan*.

Assess if the actor has done some homework. Has she memorized her lines in the sides (dialogue of the screenplay) that you provided? If she has, take note. You want actors who will do their best.

Method #4: Have the actors improvise.

I look for what the actor brings to the film. I go beyond just having actors read their lines. I get the actors to improvise, and I advise, "Don't worry about the lines. Let's just make the action of the scene clear." I need to know that actors can be spontaneous and give-and-take on the set. Further, I often film the rehearsal so I need to know that the actors are flexible and quick on the uptake.

Method #5: During the casting process, consider yourself a detective seeking to discover if the actor will be both a good team member and adept at acting.

When I run casting sessions, I talk to my receptionist, who provides me with helpful insights about how certain actors treated others. She mentioned how one actor created rapport with other actors. On the other hand, she reported that another actor treated her as "lowly help." Because my colleagues and I were concerned about the atmosphere on the set, we necessarily crossed that actor off the list.

Method #6: Show footage to other people.

Let's face it. Some people are impressive in person but

somehow are duds when seen on the screen. The solution is to show people a brief clip of three different actors. Ask: "Which actor do you prefer in this role? What worked for you?" (This is part of what I call Choice Market Testing. You provide the viewer with choices, and ask for her preference.)

Be sure that you show footage to someone in your target market.

Method #7: Realize an actor who fails to follow instructions in the audition will probably do as badly under the stressful conditions of filmmaking on the set.

My films often involve action scenes. One actor, obviously very eager, kept kicking and stepping forward, endangering her scene partner. I had directed her to stay at the far side of the room, but her wild kicks placed her partner at risk. We immediately crossed her off the list.

Method #8: Assess if you have a good rapport with the actor.

You may find a skillful actor but rapport is also a vital component of the working relationship. For example, my colleagues and I were impressed with an actor's monologue. She created powerful feelings. Unfortunately, she was abrupt with us before she began, and this created a strange energy in the room. We felt that she might be "difficult," and we crossed her off the list. If she had taken a moment to create rapport with us first, we would have seen her in a different light.

The atmosphere on the set is important. Certainly, there are times when a director is "saddled with a star"—meaning that the film will only be made with a particular star attached. However, the effective director tends to cast roles with actors he or she enjoys working with. For example, M.

Night Shyamalan often casts actress Cherry Jones in films; he probably has a great rapport with her. Director Gary Marshall frequently casts Hector Elizondo for the same reason.

Method #9: If possible, work with people with whom you hope to have a continuing good business relationship.

Our industry is based on relationships. Three years after I had met the California Motion Picture Commissioner, he helped me secure the San Luis Obispo Airport and a plane for one of my motion pictures—for free! We never know when seeds we've planted will blossom.

It is no accident that Martin Scorsese and Robert DeNiro have made a number of films together. They are comfortable with each other, and they work well together. The same is true for Tim Burton and Johnny Depp.

When you cast a film, if possible, shoot a test scene and see how you and the actor work together—over the course of three hours or more. Later, show the footage to your trusted advisors. The proof is in the work. For example, Walt Disney made a good decision to only concentrate on voices while casting the voice of Snow White. Disney avoided meeting the potential actresses face-to-face. He said that the audience would only have "the voice."

Section Five: Preproduction
17. What a Director Needs to Know About Saving Money in the Budget:

How can the director save money in the budget?

It's a matter of priorities. The director needs to identify the *Golden Scenes*. These are scenes that are crucial: the whole film rises or falls on these scenes. Reserve money and time for these scenes. Be prepared to finesse each negotiation. He or she preplans when and how to give concessions: "I must have scene 61 in the boat. But I'll give up the limousine for scene 27."

Can you save money by changing details in the script?

Yes. I saved money on one feature film when I changed "interior bus" to "interior elevator." As I mentioned elsewhere in this book, I moved the "cute meet" scene (when love interests meet each other) to an elevator. We built an elevator set in the living room of an apartment. We saved the money that would have gone to paying for the rental of a bus, security guards, extras, the driver, and special insurance.

You can save money by changing one word in a script.

One word?

Add *undercover* to police officers and you save money by avoiding wardrobe rentals or wardrobe fabrication and custom-painted patrol cars.

But there is one place I strongly advise that you avoid trying to save money. Devote significant money to the sound recording team. Bad sound is where many low budget films fall down. If you get poor sound recording on the set or on location—then the film will need to be dubbed. At that point, you lose the chance for good distribution in the United States. Film industry professionals feel that Americans will not forgive a dubbed movie (except for a dubbed animated film).

How can the director hire good crew people?

See their work. Get at least three referrals from directors who have worked with the crew person before. Interview at least three people for each position. That is a rule of thumb in business: interview at least three vendors.

Finally, each time I hire a new department head (wardrobe, photography) I tell a "printer" story about what I've learned about communicating with team members: When I self-published my first book, I hired a printer. I told the printer that my budget was small. The printer just focused on that detail and did not tell me that for merely $100 more I could have the book covers coated with varnish. It was horrible to have a box of books with covers that had ink staining my fingers! I could not sell these books.

I would have gladly found $100 more to make the books saleable. So now, I tell this "printer" story to emphasize to technical crew people that I want to know the crucial details. I'll make a decision to add to a budget, if necessary. For example, I want to know if a certain type of microphone is necessary for a scene.

Directors will often reach into their own pocket for the funds to improve their own film. Steven Spielberg devoted $5,000 of his own money to reshoot the exploding glass scene in the finale of *Close Encounters of the Third Kind*. It's a great moment in the film: The alien mothership toots a deep bass sound and the window of an observation room explodes above lead actor Richard Dreyfus.

Similarly, James Cameron reached into his own pocket to pay a portion of Kathy Bates' salary to portray Molly Brown in *Titanic*. Cameron paid $150,000 of Bates' salary requirement of $500,000.

Section Five: Production

18. What a Director Needs to Know About Leading an Actor to a Great Performance:

How can the new director help an actor give a great performance?

Ideally, the director will take an acting class at some point. Or the director will get some private coaching (which I provide for some clients).

At this point, I will give some powerful techniques to assist you in directing an actor.

The first thing to know is that each actor is different. Anthony Hopkins (*Silence of the Lambs*) has his own method: he does not want to talk much about the role. Anthony Hopkins says, "A good director will say a bit slower or faster." Similarly, Harrison Ford (*Raiders of the Lost Ark*) does not want to talk much.

On the other hand, some actors really want to "talk through the role." The effective director must focus on listening and observing. The director must interact with each actor in a unique way. The director is there to help the actors:

    a)   know where they are in the script
    b)   seize opportunities
    c)   help the actors when they feel stuck

Now, let's say you're working with novice actors. You can use a process called

focus on the objective. Some of the ideas that I will share are based on a synthesis of method acting and other acting techniques.

In each moment, an actor needs to be focused on what the character wants. This focus is the shortcut to truthful, powerful acting.

Here is a phrase that helps the actor access what the character wants:

OBJECTIVE:
I want (someone) to do (action) and I know I have it when I (see or hear) _____.

What might this look like?

"I want my father to love me and I know that he loves me when I see him wince when I tell him about a recital he missed (that I needed him to attend)."

Now, the effective director is not trying to have the actor say this phrase exactly. This objective is in the director's mind. Instead, the director can ask questions like:

a) At this minute, what do you want?
b) How do you know you have it?
c) What are you looking for that will show you that you have it?

The script might call for the father to merely ignore the son (and not wince). But as the actor portraying the son listens to his father, the "son" will be watching the "father" intently. Many novice actors are terrible at the process of listening to the other actor. Focusing on the objective helps an actor be "present in the moment."

Certain styles of acting really focus on behavior—on something that the person can act. This means, that the actor is looking for a "simple action." For example, if, as an actor, I need to cry on cue, I can place my hand on my chest (a simple action) to begin my process to reach for deep emotion.

Can you give me a few stories of directing successes?

On my feature film that went to the Cannes Film market, the lead actor was "playing one note." From the start of his monologue, he played the character as already sad. There was no place for the scene to go. I helped the actor by suggesting that the story the character recounts starts with "positive memory time." [When I say "memory time," I refer to a moment in a film when a character is caught in a moment of reliving a past memory.]

While the character remembers the start of his love relationship, a smile graces his face. Then, when he says, "And then Saigon fell, and I lost her," his energy level crashes down.

The focus of my direction of the above "then Saigon fell" dialogue scene was for the actor to avoid repeating beats. A beat relates to the rhythm and tone of a moment. To repeat a beat means to help an actor express a range of emotion through the moments—and not get stuck. Once again, the effective director helps the actor be "present in the moment."

One of my favorite times of helping an actor "find the moment" occurred when I was directing a rehearsal as I was casting a science fiction motion picture. The young woman-character was a hybrid-creature from the future. The young man-character was from the present day. I whispered one idea to the young woman. Then, I whispered a different idea to the young man. Now, when the scene played, they did not know what the other was going to do. I told the young woman: "If you could just reach over and touch the young man's arm, you could make the connection and stop the situation of losing the love of your life." I told the young man, "If she touches you, you get [a deadly disease]."

When the scene played, it broke my heart. It felt terrible to see the young woman reach to the young man, and he physically recoiled in horror. (This worked because the young woman's character was a hybrid-creature from the future.)

This is similar to Alfred Hitchcock's technique for a scene of *Rear Window*. A couple is taking their mattress off the fire escape. Alfred Hitchcock secretly told the man to pull the mattress to one window—and Hitchcock told the woman to pull toward the other window. The spontaneous tug-of-war makes a funny scene ending with the man tumbling into a window.

SECTION SIX: PRODUCTION

19. What a Director Needs to Know About Leading Others

How does a new director learn to effectively lead people?

We learn by doing. I strongly suggest that the new director direct a one-minute film. Start small. Get practical experience. It helps when the director creates a comfortable atmosphere on the set. Steven Spielberg says, "A good director knows when to say 'yes.'" I add that a good director creates an atmosphere where you have a lot to say 'yes' to.

How do you create that good atmosphere?

You help people feel calm. Wolfgang Peterson (director of *Air Force One*) has a break for soup at 11 AM (it's a European custom).

Clint Eastwood (director of *Million Dollar Baby*) has a quiet set. No one yells "Quiet on the set!" No one yells "action." There is no loud clapping of the clapperboard (the board that snaps when the assistant says "Take One" – and 'snap'). Clint Eastwood merely twirls his index finger which silently alerts his camera operator and sound recordist to roll film and roll tape. Clint never says "Cut." He just says, "That's enough."

On my set, I have the camera roll and I say to the actors "Whenever you're ready." For tough emotional scenes, I will do an "end slate." That means, we use the clapperboard (placed upside-down) at the end of the scene. The value of an "end slate" is that the actor does not enter a scene disrupted by the slam of the clapperboard. The upside-down clapperboard alerts the editor that the sync point for sound is at the end of the scene.

When I talk with an actor, we have a quiet conversation to the side. I never embarrass a team member in front of other people. I first start with "what works." I'll say, "I like how you're really listening to Mark when he says, 'My house tilted—'"

Then, I'll say things like:
- "What if we try . . ."
- "Are we missing an opportunity here?"
- "I agree that XY is important, and when we add..."

You notice that I say "and." If a person says "but," it will make the words before "but" sound insincere.

When a department head—like art director, special effects specialist, etc. comes to me with a new idea, I often reply: "I'm going to ponder that." Or I say, "Let me stir that in my soup." I do not reject ideas quickly. Any idea can be a springboard for really great improvement. It is important not to reject ideas quickly or with a negative tone because that would teach crew members to avoid offering ideas. The effective director creates a good atmosphere where people feel comfortable to offer ideas.

You need to praise people, but some people can't believe praise. So you need to be specific and say something like: "I really appreciate when you did 1-2-3, and that helps us accomplish XY. Good work." Also encourage your creative team to come up with solutions. This is called completed staff work—a process in which you ask for:

a)   Three alternatives
b)   The person's endorsement of one alternative
c)   The person's reason for endorsing one of the alternatives

Often, I respond "I agree. Go forward with that one."

Is there a way to deliver a criticism effectively?

Sometimes I use a straw man to convey an idea that may not be welcome. In this context, I designate a straw man as a fictitious person who may have trouble with the work being reviewed. I might say. "I have one concern. I'm wondering how someone from the middle of the country, who has never been to San Francisco, would react to the image in Storyboard 257. Would it turn them off like a light? How can we do something to make it work for that person?"

SECTION SEVEN: POSTPRODUCTION

20. What a Director Needs to Know About Editing:

Can the director solve production problems in the editing room?

Yes, that often happens. I have a list of 12 Editing Solutions to Filming Problems [that I first revealed in my book *Darkest Secrets of the Film and Television Industry Every Actor Should Know*].

Snatch Victory from the Jaws of Production Defeat (What to do when the shots don't turn out how you want them to)

The following is a brief overview of solutions you can use when you are disappointed with what you filmed. Think of this as a Quick List. These items were included in the Final Exam I gave my digital filmmaking students at Cogswell Polytechnical College in Silicon Valley.

Editing Solutions to Filming Problems:
1. Reframe the shot.

To reframe is to adjust the frame of the image of your shot. You can use your digital editing software to zoom-in to eliminate distracting shadows for example. Television and the Internet are often referred to as "close-up mediums." That is, since the screen is smaller, a close-up shot provides more impact.

In addition, be careful about how far you zoom in. At a certain point, the pixels start to get distracting.

2. Add motion.

You can use your digital editing software to do a zoom-in or a pan across the image of your shot. You can adjust the shot to do both types of motion at the same time. A number of documentaries make a photograph "come alive" by a zoom-in or a pan-across motion.

3. Use sound to cover some error or add A.D.R. or atmosphere.

Often, sound can be your Band-aid solution. For example, one error could be that not enough extras arrived on a particular day. You can film the shots closer in and later add atmosphere—the sounds of clinking glasses and conversation to give us the illusion that the scene takes place in a crowded restaurant. You can add A.D.R. (Automatic Dialogue Replacement), which means to add dialogue in the sound studio. With A.D.R., you can add a crucial bit of dialogue that helps you fill in a gap in the script.

4. Use music.

Let's say you have a romantic scene between the leading

man and woman. The dialogue didn't go as planned. You can use music and a few shots of the two people walking and talking to imply that they are becoming closer.

5. Cutaway fast.

To cutaway is to edit so that the shot you are on is shorter. George Lucas used quick cuts in the original release of *Star Wars: A New Hope (Episode IV)* (the first feature film starring Mark Hamill, Harrison Ford and Carrie Fisher). George Lucas cut away from a matte painting after a second or two so the audience would not have time to realize "Oh, that's not real; it's just a painting of parked space ships." Our goal is to give just an impression of the idea or image. Cutaway fast also when you have a weak actor. For example, let's say you need to show a surprise reaction shot. If your actor overacts, cut the shot early when their eyes are just starting to go wide in surprise.

6. Cut on the action (hide the cut).

Here's an example of hiding the cut. In a wideshot, a waiter walks past a table. In a closer shot, the waiter is seen walking past again. When putting these two shots together, you can make the cut feel "seamless" (or hide the cut) by having the waiter begin a move in the wideshot and complete it in the medium shot.

7. Use a visual motif.

The feature film *Mash* appeared like a jumbled, episodic mess in the first rough cut. Then director Robert Altman added the visual motif of the loud speakers as "the glue" between sections. This gave the film unity and rhythm. In one of my feature films, we used a rose as a continuing visual motif.

8. Devise your pick-up shot (use a stand-in).

In my feature film that went to the Cannes Film Festival market, the lead actress was unavailable for a reshoot. I had another actress work as a stand-in. In the final edit, I had a shot of the lead actress walk in the door. Then there was a close-up in which the leading man looked up. Then, an over-the-shoulder shot showed the stand-in's back. It became a great opportunity to see the leading man's reaction to the new line created in the editing room: "I've been rehearsing this act for a show. I don't know if it works. Would you be my first audience?"

9. Revisit your throughline.

The throughline of your project is the "spine" of the script. For the original *Star Wars* film, it was "make preparations and then destroy the Death Star."

If your rough cut is not working, revisit your throughline. Perhaps too much time has passed between moments where the audience is reminded: "this is what is at stake here."

Here is an example of making a film work by revisiting the throughline. For one of my films, I added a scene in which the main character "David" calls his sweetheart from a payphone. An element of the throughline is that David must tell her that he is out of remission from the disease he suffers. But he stops himself and says, "Oh, there's my bus." There is no bus, and "David" (and the audience) is disappointed in him.

10. Revisit your bookends.

Bookends are the process of beginning your project with a startling opening image, and then completing the project with a final image that is a twist on the original image. Here's an example. For one of my films, I began with the image of a man's face as the character falls onto a concrete sidewalk. In the next shot, he gets up, apparently okay. At the end of the film, I show the original shot of the man falling on the sidewalk. The twist is now there is a growing puddle of blood issuing from the man. The shot was further intensified by falling rain. Apparently, the whole film was a glimpse of the man's final, imaginative thoughts before his death.

When you revisit your bookends, you identify what your "twist" is and you think of some images you can place in the middle of your project that support your film's conclusion.

11. Borrow from another scene or from trims or outtakes.

One of my favorite transitions in my feature film that went to the Cannes Film Festival market utilizes an outtake. We filmed a scene with a car coming towards the camera at night. The headlights flashed the camera. I used that flash as a transition to a morning shot. Here's how it went: a) exterior shot of car coming towards the camera, b) flash of headlights, c) additional bright white light added in editing, and d) flash of white dissolves away to reveal the car's interior with the driver talking to his companion the next morning.

Here is an example of borrowing from a trim (excess footage cut from a shot). In *Field of Dreams*, the director Phil Alden Robinson needed a shot of Ray Liotta looking upon Kevin Costner in an expectant way. Phil did not have the reaction shot. He borrowed a trim from a shot where Ray was just getting ready to catch a baseball. Cut into the scene, the shot now makes it look like Ray's body language is telling Kevin: "Well, what's it going to be? Are you going to take action? I'm ready if you do take action."

12. Use a match cut or montage.

You create a match cut when you use a motion or shape from two different locations to make a smooth cut. You match the motion or shape. On one project, I wanted to connect two different chase scenes. In the first shot the hero is running from a speeding motorcycle. In the second shot, the hero rides a jet ski chased by a pursuing jet ski. The match cut begins with the hero looking back at the motorcycle, then CUT, and the hero completes turning his head to look forward (but now he's on the jet ski with a different pursuer).

A montage is similar to how a number of music videos use a sequence of shots. You cut images together to give an impression such as: "The man and woman are devoting time together and becoming close friends." Many feature films have a song (of course, on the music soundtrack album!) placed over a montage.

You can use this Quick List to bring up your spirits when you feel disappointed when viewing the dailies or rushes (unedited footage) of your project. The above 12 Solutions can help you make your project work.

What about breaking the rules?

First, know what the rules are. For example, one rule of editing is to wait until a moving shot stops before cutting to a different angle with a stationary camera. In my feature film that went to the Cannes Film market, I purposely cut from a moving shot to a stationary camera shot on the line: "We get deported, okay!" The jarring cut emphasized the jarring emotion.

This leads us to the question: How do you "break the

rules effectively?"

Here are helpful ideas:

- First, have an excellent beginning to clue us into the nature of the film—especially if the film involves more than one genre.
- Second, have some well thought out foreshadowing elements.
- Third, have good transitions into the next phase—or next change in tone.
- Fourth, separate the character functions. For example, in *Star Wars: Episode IV—A New Hope*, Han Solo is the rogue, Luke is the fresh-faced young hero - and at times, C3PO and R2D2 are the Laurel and Hardy comedic relief team.
- Fifth, do test screenings of your rough cut to see if an audience flows with your transitions.

SECTION EIGHT: MARKETING—FUNDRAISING—DISTRIBUTION

21. What a Director Needs to Know About Marketing—Fundraising—Distribution

Tell me about marketing.

Focusing on your target market is important as you work on the screenplay – whether you are the screenwriter or you are working with a screenwriter. Come up with the scene that you will use as a filmclip if you are on a talk show (for example, *The Tonight Show*). Create a scene that embodies the entertainment value/emotional impact of your feature film.

Many filmmakers talk about how they are their own audience. I also suggest that early on, you cut together a rough draft commercial of your film. You can use storyboards. The point is that you are focused on the central ideas of the film. I have a phrase: *How your market it changes how you make it*. Carl Foreman, producer/screenwriter of

High Noon, said that a film needs a chariot race (like the race in *Ben Hur*). He meant that a film needs something so great that people talk about it on the way home from the movie theater. Also, create two versions of the movie poster. Then use what I call *Choice Market Testing*. Go to people and ask:

- "Based on this poster, which movie would you pay to see?"
- "What about your preference grabs you?"

The following is a lightly edited transcript of an interview:

Tom, in our short time together, let's cover the highlights and some techniques you used to move your feature films forward. We'll cover topics from script to fundraising . . . to the set . . . and finally distribution.

I'm glad to be supportive of new filmmakers in making their dreams come true.

How can a new screenwriter break through writer's block?

When I sit down to write a first draft, I just write. If I get stuck, I follow the procedure that best-selling author Piers Anthony uses. Like him, I use brackets – and I "talk" to myself in between the brackets. For example, I might type "[I know that in the first 10 minutes, Susan needs to come across a clue that will help her solve the situation. What would that clue be? Could it be a letter? A missing photo on the wall?]" In this way, I think out loud and into my laptop computer. Just by doing this process, I avoid writer's block.

The big question is how do you raise money for your film project?

To raise funds you need two things: 1) establish your credibility and 2) provide a preview of the film. To gain credibility, make sure that you note in your business plan how you have previously completed projects with successful outcomes. Also, when I raised money for my first feature film, I had already gained credibility by winning various awards for short films.

About providing a preview of the film, what I mean is that you give the person a feeling of the value of the film. Give a feeling of how marketable the film is. For example, when I begin a film project, I design a poster. Sometimes, I commission music so that the energy of the film can be experienced.

For example, with my *TimePulse* trilogy of motion pictures project (http://www.TimePulse.com), I wrote the first book *TimePulse: Beyond Titanic* (available at Amazon.com and BarnesandNoble.com). My team is also working on a graphic novel. The images from the graphic novel form the pre-production storyboards. All of these details add up to give the potential investor an experience of the value of the proposed film.

To raise funds, identify your community, that is, the people who care about your subject matter. Follow director Spike Lee's example. When he ran out of funds for *Malcolm X*, he went to Bill Cosby and Oprah Winfrey for additional funding.

When directing on the set, what mistake does the novice director need to avoid?

The mistake would be trying to relate to every person in the same way. For example, Harrison Ford praised director Sydney Pollack (*Out of Africa*) for his ability to direct each person in a different, specific and appropriate way. Certainly when one directs a no-nonsense person like Harrison Ford, using a minimum of words is advisable. However, some actors like to really talk through a part. So the mistake to avoid is being so busy with technical details that you forget to observe each actor's preferences. Make sure to do little things so that each actor knows that you care.

Many new filmmakers are afraid to be exploited when they seek distribution. What do you suggest?

I suggest studying reputable books to understand the business side of the industry. It's important to realize that a filmmaker needs to walk carefully. When I was presented with a distribution contract for one of my feature films, I took an audio recorder and noted 47 points to which I would not agree. I worked with my attorney, and I had about 97% of the points modified; the distributor would not move on the remaining 3%. If you are working with a smaller distributor, make sure that the contract specifies that you retain ownership of your film. There are tragic stories of small distributors taking the ownership rights, and then going out of business—and then the filmmaker can never retrieve the film. Certainly, it's necessary to get an appropriate attorney to protect your interests.

To attract a distributor be sure to make it easy for the distributor to understand how your film can be marketed and who the target market is. For one of my feature films, I met 80 distributors at an industry event, showed them a collage of images from the film, and asked them if this film was the type of film they would distribute. I had 20 videotapes with me. And I only gave tapes to those distributors who were a match.

Tom, we're out of time. What final details would you like to share with new filmmakers?

We live in a terrific time for filmmaking. You can get HD video camera for a modest price and start filming next week. Robert Rodriguez (director of *Once Upon A Time in Mexico*) said that everyone has 12 lousy films in them. My addition to this comment is: "If that's true, make 12 one-minute films. And practice and learn your craft."

CONCLUSION:
Here are the six secrets shared in this interview.

1. Break writer's block by "talking to yourself in between brackets."

2. To raise funds, establish your credibility by showing how you've completed projects with successful outcomes.

3. Also, to raise funds, give people a preview experience of the film.

4. On the set, direct each actor according to the person's preferences.

5. To gain distribution, develop a page of images to show potential distributors how the film can be marketed.

6. When you receive the distribution agreement, go through it carefully and engage an attorney to protect your interests.

A FINAL WORD AND THE SPRINGBOARD TO YOUR DREAMS

Congratulations on your efforts with this book.

I'm grateful for this opportunity to provide these insights so you can leap forward to making your dreams come true.

We have covered:

Section One: 21 Darkest Secrets of Film Directing (and Your Countermeasures)

Section Two: Use the D.I.R.E.C.T. System

Section Three: Make the Screenplay Excellent

Section Four: Develop the Film Project

Section Five: Preproduction

Section Six: Production

Section Seven: Post Production

Section Eight: Marketing—Fundraising—Distribution

To gain more value from this book, be sure to go through it and develop your own To Do List. Take some action. Any action towards improving skills and promoting yourself is helpful. I often say, "Better than zero."

Please consider gaining special training through my coaching (phone and in-person), workshops and presentations.

Note the other eight books in this series...

- Darkest Secrets of Making a Pitch to the Film and Television Industry
- Darkest Secrets of Film Directing
- Darkest Secrets of Charisma
- Darkest Secrets of Persuasion and Seduction Masters: How to Protect Yourself and Turn the Power to Good
- Darkest Secrets of Business Communication: Using Your Personal Brand
- Darkest Secrets of Small Business Marketing
- Darkest Secrets of Spiritual Seduction Masters
- Darkest Secrets of Negotiation Masters

See my blog at
www.BeHeardandBeTrusted.com

The best to you and may your filmmaking dreams come true.
Tom
Tom Marcoux,
Motion Picture Director, Actor, Producer, Screenwriter
America's Communication Coach
P.S. View the 8 Other *Darkest Secrets* books:
See **Free Chapters** of Tom Marcoux's 19 books
at http://amzn.to/ZiCTRj

Titles include:
Be Heard and Be Trusted
Nothing Can Stop You This Year

Truth No One Will Tell You
10 Seconds to Wealth
Your Secret Charisma
Wake Up Your Spirit to Prosperity
The Cat Advantage
— and more.
(For coaching, reach Tom Marcoux
 at tomsupercoach@gmail.com)

EXCERPT FROM
DARKEST SECRETS OF THE FILM AND TELEVISION INDUSTRY EVERY ACTOR SHOULD KNOW:
A FILM DIRECTOR AND ACTOR REVEALS SECRETS FOR YOUR ACTING, AUDITIONS, MOVIE ROLES AND SELF-PROMOTION

(plus How to Make Your Video for YouTube.com and Webisodes)

2nd Edition by Tom Marcoux

BOOK I: DARKEST SECRETS OF THE FILM AND TELEVISION INDUSTRY EVERY ACTOR SHOULD KNOW (AND YOUR COUNTERMEASURES) —CHAPTER 1

What do you really hope for with your acting career? Perhaps you want to feel the thrill of acting on the set of major feature films or in top productions on Broadway. Or you want to make top money appearing in television shows. Maybe you simply enjoy the adventure of expressing emotion as a variety of characters. Perhaps you continue to feel the hunger to perform since you were a teen.

Imagine that you could learn the real pitfalls and effective countermeasures to the tough parts of an acting career. Those answers wait within the pages of this book.

This book reveals *21 Darkest Secrets of the Film and Television Industry Every Actor Should Know.* More than that, it provides you with countermeasures so you'll do the right things to protect your career and leap forward to make your dreams come true. The section Book II provides a guide for producing and directing your own video for YouTube.com and webisodes. Producing your own short video helps you get essential demonstration footage (that helps one gain acting roles). Book III provides 25 secrets to self-promotion.

How did I come to write this book? As an actor and director of feature films and other work I have been on both sides of the audition table. So I'll pull back the curtain and reveal what directors are thinking during your audition. One of the feature films I directed (and had a lead role in) went to the Cannes Film market and gained international distribution. I've acted in feature films, commercials and more (projects headlined by Chris O'Donnell, Ricardo Montalban, and others). And I've taught workshops on acting and self-promotion.

Some of my former college students posted messages at Facebook about how tough it was to endure the film and television industry. Some of them were even quitting. I wanted to help. You see, I currently teach public speaking and science fiction cinema/literature to graduate students and college students. So I did not have the chance to teach those former college students the material contained in this book.

And now I am here, as your coach, to help you strengthen yourself and to help you overcome pitfalls of an acting career so you keep pursuing your dreams.

Let's begin . . .

DARKEST SECRET #1: FILM AND TV PEOPLE HAVE LONG MEMORIES AND THEY GET EVEN

After I ran some auditions, I went to my receptionist and asked about how a particular actor "Samuel" treated her and other actors. She gave me the news about Samuel's crass behavior and how he belittled everyone in the waiting room. I added that to my other observations and necessarily crossed Samuel off the list.

When you come across as friendly and professional, you get more offers and opportunities to audition. But a number of actors walk around moody. One of my filmmaking colleagues, a producer, said, "We want professionals; we don't want babies."

Throughout this book, I'll reveal subtle mistakes actors can make, seemingly innocent actions that create manifestly wrong impressions. A director told a friend of mine about how an actor who had the role at the end of his audition—until he asked to drink from one of the casting directors' water bottles.

For more insight, here is an excerpt from an interview with Casting Director Randi Acton.

Near the end of the interview, Randi reveals how some casting directors appear to "get even." In this interview,

Randi speaks about parents and child actors. However, there is much that any actor can gain from the straight forward advice Randi gives.

Tom: What are ideal qualifications for parents of child actors?

Randi: Parents [and all actors] need to be cooperative. Just pleasant to work with. The entertainment business is extremely stressful and very long hours. Everybody on a production is tired. So when you come on the set you want to be [pleasant] . . .

Tom: If there's only one thing you can tell a child actor that will help her get the part, what is it?

Randi: Just be yourself. I tell kids that there are apples and oranges. And a director, in his head, is looking for an apple. You come in, and you're the most talented, gorgeous, most adorable, charismatic orange. He adores you, but you're not an apple. So, it's not personal. Kids really have to know that if you don't get cast, it doesn't mean you're not talented. It just means you're an orange instead of an apple. It's as simple as that. Sometimes, he's looking for an apple, and you really are an incredible orange, and all of a sudden, he switches in his mind: "I don't want an apple. I changed my mind. I want an orange." And you get the part.

Tom: That's what happened to me. In two feature films I have directed, the part was written as a boy. And a girl came in – and the role changed to a girl. Both times!

Randi: I remember! Because what you saw ended up being what you needed. But you didn't know it until you saw it.

Tom: Tell me about how parents help or hinder their children.

Randi: On one film project, we ended up with a [name

actor's son]. It didn't matter that he was the well-known actor's son. "Joey" [not his real name] was just brilliant. So he got the part. . . [Then,] we get this girl that's just incredible. And even Joey said, "That's who I want." They had a relationship because they did callbacks together. Their chemistry together was incredible. So everything is perfect. Everything is great. They come to the set, and the girl turns into a complete nightmare. Her acting was brilliant. Her look was great. She became this overnight, stuck-up, little star at a young age. It was a major nightmare. The girl was difficult. Someone went up to her and asked, "What part are you playing?" She replied, "I'm the star!" It got to where we were sick to our stomachs. And her mother didn't handle that at all. Her mother was just as bad. There was a big fight between the mothers. . . I will never cast her again [as a child]. And I'm sure that the parents have no idea . . . . If the parents are difficult, I will not cast the kid again. We have enough headaches and enough emergency things to deal with. We want to work with actors that are easy to work with. I'd take an actor that is easy to work with even over a talented actor that's a snob. On another film, an adult was complaining about the size of her trailer. She made it a big problem. She was calling her manager . . . She is famous, but I won't cast her again. I won't put up with that. There are too many nice people in the world, who are also talented and not stuck up. I've talked with other casting directors, and most of us don't put up with that."

[The rest of the interview with Casting Director Randi Acton is in *Book IV* of this book.]

* * *

At Hollywood gatherings, I have repeatedly heard a number of people saying: "I won't put up with that." Casting directors say, "I won't work with that actor again. I won't put up with that." And I hear actors say, "I finally fired my agent." Film industry people, under so much pressure, seek to relieve it by avoiding people who rub them the wrong way.

For example, Ed Harris, while acting in James Cameron's *The Abyss* nicknamed the film "The Abuse." Ed said that he felt traumatized from the filmmaking and found himself crying in the car on his way back to the hotel. Ed also said that he would never again work with James Cameron.

Earlier I spoke of film and television people having long memories. In 1999, George Clooney had an argument with director David O. Russell on the set of *Three Kings*. The words led to punches. To this day, George Clooney maintains that he will never work with Russell again.

As I discuss the Darkest Secrets in this book, every section will include countermeasures so that you do the right things for your own career. For example, one countermeasure for this section is: avoid causing directors, producers and casting people problems. Make sure to have some positive interactions.

Directors, producers and casting people only like to hire people who make their lives easier.

For example, Steven Spielberg made the following movies with Michael Kahn as his editor: *Lincoln, The Adventures of Tintin, Indiana Jones and the Kingdom of the Crystal Skull, Munich, War of the Worlds, The Terminal, Catch Me if You Can, Minority Report, A.I, Artificial Intelligence, Saving Private Ryan, Amistad, The Lost World: Jurassic Park, Schindler's List, Jurassic Park, Hook, Always, Indiana Jones and the Last Crusade, Empire of the Sun, The Color Purple, Indiana Jones and the Temple of*

Doom, Raiders of the Lost Ark, 1941, and *Close Encounters of the Third Kind.*

Steven Spielberg enlisted John Williams as the composer of the music soundtracks for all of the above films except *The Color Purple.*

Points to Remember:

- **Darkest Secret #1: Film and TV people have long memories and they get even.**

- **Your Countermeasure:**

Avoid causing directors, producers and casting people problems. Make some friends or at least have some positive interactions. Remember, film and television people are extremely busy, stressed out and tired people. They label co-workers quickly. They only like to hire people who make their lives easier.

CHAPTER 2
DARKEST SECRET #2: YOU CAN'T "GET IN" THE INDUSTRY UNTIL YOU PROVE YOURSELF (BUT YOU CAN TAKE MATTERS INTO YOUR OWN HANDS)

Industry people talk about how, in many cases, you can't get significant roles in film and television unless you're a SAG actor (Screen Actors Guild) or have an agent. However, many agents don't look at actors who are not with SAG. This is an apparent Catch-22.

There is a solution to the above conundrum. Do

something, in a small way, that demonstrates your skill (which can lead to roles in independent films and more). Numerous people are using the Internet, and YouTube.com in particular, to gain attention and jump start their careers. For example, singer/songwriter Dave Carroll felt both injury and insult when United Airlines baggage handlers broke his guitar. United Airlines personnel said that the company would not make restitution. Dave replied that if they did not fix his guitar, he would make and post three music videos on YouTube. The videos would expose the problems of the broken guitar and his disappointment about United's refusal to fix the guitar. As of this writing, the music video and song "United Breaks Guitars" has had 13,006,164 views on YouTube.com. It is likely that Dave Carroll has gotten a lot of gigs due to the video. He even authored a book titled *United Breaks Guitars: The Power of One Voice in the Age of Social Media*.

Actress Felicia Day took action and created a webisodes series entitled *The Guild*. And this action led to her starring in at least 13 episodes of the TV Series *Eureka*. Here's how she describes the process (at her website):

"There are a few times in life when you REALLY get rewarded for working hard. That is the story of why I am playing 'Dr. Holly Martin' on *Eureka* [TV series]. The exec producer Amy Berg and showrunner Jamie Paglia were aware of my work on the web (because they are awesome, true geeks themselves) and they actually CREATED this role for me. Yep, no Hollywood agents, no horrific auditions where I cry in the car afterwards, they simply called me in for a meeting and basically created the funnest character I've ever played. And KEPT writing her in! The great thing about Eureka is that it's a wonderful balance of quirky comedy and drama, the exact tone and sensibility I love to play. And the crew is truly wonderful. So seriously, it couldn't be a bigger dream come true to be flying back and forth to Vancouver and playing around with what I like to call my Canadian family now. As of this writing, I've done 13 episodes over seasons 4 and 5."

Regarding Felicia Day's web series *The Guild:*
"*The Guild* [now in its fifth season] is a independent sitcom web series about a group of online gamers. The show started in the late summer of 2007, and for the first season was financed solely by PayPal donations from LOYAL FANS. Since season 2, The Guild has been distributed by Xbox Live and Microsoft and sponsored by Sprint. Episodes vary from 3-8 minutes in length, and follow the Guild members' lives online and offline. "The Guild" has won numerous awards, including the SXSW, YouTube and Yahoo Web Series Awards in 2008, and 3 Streamy Awards in 2009: Best Comedy Web Series, Best Ensemble, and Best Actress for Felicia Day." [from watchtheguild.com]

Years ago, Billy Bob Thornton proved to the film industry that he could act when he wrote, directed and starred in the feature film *Sling Blade*. Similarly, Bruce Campbell produced and starred in the first low budget feature film *The Evil Dead*, which was directed by his friend Sam Raimi. Bruce's career took off after that first feature film led to two sequels, television show guest appearances, playing the lead in the TV series *The Adventures of Brisco County, Jr.*, and leading roles in other feature films. Currently, Bruce co-stars on the hit TV series *Burn Notice*.

The above four examples reveal that you can do something to forward your career. You can cast yourself. Produce your own short film first. And consider producing your own web series or feature film.

To demonstrate your acting skills (and simultaneously improve them), you could produce short films and place them on YouTube.com and you can embed the films on a page at your own actor website. In a later section of this book entitled *BOOK II: Taking Control of Your Career: Producing Your Own Short Film, Feature Film or Web Series*, I will share numerous strategies that my colleagues and I have developed through hard-won experience.

End of Excerpt from
Darkest Secrets of the Film and Television Industry Every Actor Should Know
Copyright 2013 Tom Marcoux Media, LLC

Purchase your copy of this book at Amazon.com or BarnesandNoble.com
See **Free Chapters** of Tom Marcoux's 19 books at http://amzn.to/ZiCTRj

ABOUT THE AUTHOR

Tom Marcoux helps people like you fulfill big dreams. Known as America's Communication Coach, Tom has authored 19 books with sales in 15 countries. One of his *Darkest Secrets* books rose to #1 on Amazon.com Hot New Releases in Business Life (and in Business Communication). He guides clients and audiences (IBM, Sun Microsystems, etc.) to success in job interviewing, public speaking, media relations, and branding. A member of the National Speakers Association, he is a professional coach and guest expert on TV, radio, and print, and was dubbed "the Personal Branding Instructor" by the *San Francisco Examiner*. Tom addressed National Assoc. of Broadcasters' Conference six years running. With a degree in psychology, Tom is a guest lecturer at **Stanford University**, DeAnza, & California State University, and teaches public speaking, science fiction cinema/literature and comparative religion at Academy of Art University. Winner of a special award at the **Emmys**, Tom wrote, directed, and produced a feature film that the distributor took to the **Cannes film market**, and the film gained international distribution. He is engaged in book/film projects *Crystal Pegasus* (children's) and *TimePulse* (science fiction). See TomSuperCoach.com and Tom's well-received blog at www.BeHeardandBeTrusted.com

Tom Marcoux can help you with **speech writing** and **coaching for your best performance.**
As Tom says, *Make Your Speech a Pleasant Beach.*
Join Tom's Linkedin.com group: *Executive Public Speaking and Communication Power.*
Get a **Free** report: "9 Deadly Mistakes to Avoid for Your Next Speech and 9 Surefire Methods" at

http://tomsupercoach.com/freereport9Mistakes4Speech.html

Tom Marcoux has trained CEOs, small business owners, and graduate students to speak with impact and gain audiences' tremendous approval and cooperation. *Learn how to present and get thunderous applause!*

"Tom, Thanks for your coaching and work with me on revising my speech at a major university. Working with you has been so enlightening for me. Through your gentle prodding and guidance I was able to write a speech that connects with the audience. I wish everyone could experience the transformation I have undergone. You have helped me discover the warm and compelling stories that now make my speech reach hearts and uplift minds. This was truly an empowering experience. I cannot thank you enough for your great assistance." — J.S.

Become a fan of Tom's graphic novels/feature films:

Science fiction: *TimePulse*
www.facebook.com/timepulsegraphicnovel

Fantasy Thriller: *Jack AngelSword*
type "JackAngelSword" at Facebook.com

Children's Fantasy: *Crystal Pegasus*
www.facebook.com/crystalpegasusandrose

See **Free Chapters** of Tom Marcoux's 19 books at http://amzn.to/ZiCTRj

Special Offer Just for Readers of this Book:

Contact Tom Marcoux at tomsupercoach@gmail.com for special discounts on books, coaching, workshops and presentations. Just mention your experience with this book.